Using and Understanding Maps

Industry of the World

Consulting Editor

Scott E. Morris
College of Mines and Earth Resources
University of Idaho

Chelsea House Publishers
New York   Philadelphia

This Publication was designed, edited and computer generated by
Lovell Johns Limited
10 Hanborough Business Park
Long Hanborough
Witney
Oxon, England OX8 8LH

The contents of this volume are based on the latest data available at the
time of publication.

Map credit: *Antarctica source map prepared at 1:20,000 by the British
Antarctic Survey Mapping and Geographic Information Centre, 1990.*

Cover credit: *Dick Durrance/Woodfin Camp and Associates.*

Printed in Mexico

3 5 7 9 8 6 4 2

Library of Congress Cataloging in Publication Data

Industry of the world/editorial consultant, Scott Morris:
       p. cm.—(Using and understanding maps)
       Includes glossary and index/gazetteer.
       Includes bibliographical references.
       Summary: Eighteen map spreads highlight the economic activity
around the world.
       ISBN 0-7910-1807-5. — ISBN 0-7910-1820-2 (pbk.)
       1. Industry—Maps. 2. Economic geography—Maps.
       [1. Industry—Maps, 2. Economic geography—Maps, 3. Atlases.]
       I. Morris, Scott Edward. II. Series.
       G1046.G1I46 1993 <G&M>
       338.' .0022' 3 — dc20   92-22288
                                  CIP
                                  MAP AC

Introduction

We inhabit a fascinating and mysterious planet where the earth's physical features, life-forms, and the diversity of human culture conspire to produce a breathtaking environment. We don't have to travel very far to see and experience the wealth of this diverse planet; in fact, we don't have to travel at all. Everywhere images of the world are abundantly available in books, newspapers, magazines, movies, television, and the arts. We could say that *everywhere* one looks, our world is a brilliant moving tapestry of shapes, colors, and textures, and our experience of its many messages — whether in our travels or simply by gazing out into our own backyards — is what we call reality.

Geography is the study of a portion of that reality. More so, it is the study of how the physical and biological components (rocks, animals, plants, and people) of our planet are distributed and how they are interconnected. Geographers seek to describe and to explain the physical patterns that have evolved on the earth and also to discover the significance in the ways they have evolved. To do this, geographers rely on maps.

Maps can be powerful images. They convey selective information about vast areas of an overwhelmingly cluttered world. The cartographer, or mapmaker, must carefully choose the theme of a map, that is, what it will show, knowing that a good map will convey the essence of information while at the same time making the information easy to comprehend.

This volume and its companions in UNDERSTANDING AND USING MAPS are about the planet we call earth and the maps we use to find our way along its peaks and valleys. Each volume displays map images that reveal how the world is arranged according to a specific theme such as population, industries or the endangered world. The maps in each volume are accompanied by an interesting collection of facts — some are rather obvious, others are oddities. Yet all are meant to be informative.

Along with a wealth of facts, there are explanations of the various attributes and phenomena depicted by the maps. This information is provided to better understand the significance of the maps as well as to demonstrate how the many themes relate.

Names for places are essential to geographers. To study the world without devising names for places would be extremely difficult. But geographers also know that names are in no way permanent; place names change as people change. The recent reunification of Germany and the breakup of what was the Soviet Union — events that seem colossal from the perspective of socioeconomics — to geographers are simply events that require the drawing or erasing of one or a few boundaries and the renaming of one or several land masses. The geographer is constantly reminded that the world is in flux; a map is always in danger of being rendered obsolete by a turn in current events.

Because the world is dynamic, it continues to captivate the mind and stimulate the imagination. USING AND UNDERSTANDING MAPS presents the world as it is today, with the reservation that any dramatic rearrangement of land and people is likely, indeed inevitable, thus requiring the making of a new map. In this way maps are themselves a part of the evolutionary process.

Scott E. Morris

Our lives have been completely transformed by industry. It is difficult to conceive of living through a single day without industrial products. There would be no automobiles, refrigeration, plumbing, electricity, radio, television, telephone — not even foods grown and harvested in distant places. Industry makes a highly visible imprint on the earth and the lives and expectations of human beings.

Cultural geographers and historians recognize two great "revolutions" in human history. The purposeful planting and harvesting of food and the raising of livestock, as opposed to the hunting of wild animals and the gathering of plants, is referred to as the "agriculture revolution." The second, the "industrial revolution," began in Great Britain in the early 1700s, when water power was first employed to drive the looms of the textile industry. From these humble beginnings, industrialization has spread over nearly the entire world.

With the development of the steam engine, the face of the planet was changed forever. The steam engine brought about the railroad, and for the first time in history materials could be cheaply transported across great distances in enormous quantities. This allowed industries to locate away from sources of raw materials and also to deliver finished goods to distant markets at reasonable prices. Then came the internal combustion gasoline engine, the electric motor, and the jet turbine. Today, our transportation network of highways, railroads, waterways, and airways hums with the continual movement of raw materials and finished goods that are the lifeblood of modern civilization.

Geographers distinguish between primary, secondary, and tertiary industries. *Primary industries* are those engaged in extracting resources through activities such as mining, agriculture, forestry, and fishing. Making these raw materials into finished goods is the job of *secondary industries*. We often refer to this process as manufacturing, although there are usually many steps involved. The "product" of one secondary industry, (a steel mill, for example) is raw material to another secondary industry (the automobile manufacturer). Just think for a minute of all the goods you might encounter in an average day, and you will get some idea of the number of secondary industries. *Tertiary industries* are commonly called service industries because no tangible goods are produced. Instead, a service is provided. The transportation and communication industries are good examples, as are banking, insurance, health care, and education.

These distinctions are often blurred, however, because many companies may be owned by a single corporation called a conglomerate. In addition, many conglomerates operate all over the world. Multinational or transnational corporations have become increasingly important in the global economy because they control both the latest technology and the large amounts of money necessary to efficiently extract raw materials, manufacture goods cheaply, and deliver them at a competitive price.

Through these multinational corporations, the face of traditional industrial geography is changing. The patterns you see on the following pages are really signs of another industrial revolution in progress. In today's world of instantaneous communication, information sharing, and global manufacturing and marketing, there is a new freedom displayed by industry. An integrated global economy, a new economic order, is emerging that will break down the political subdivisions of the traditional nation-states.

Scott E. Morris

egend lists and explains the symbols and colors
d on the map. It is called a legend because it
s the story of a map. It is important to read the
p legend to find out exactly what the symbols
an because some symbols do not look like
at they represent. For example, a dot stands
a town.
ery map in this atlas has a legend on it.

This legend lists and explains the colors and
symbols used on the map on that page only.
The legend on the left, below, shows examples of the
colors used on the maps in all the atlases in this
series. Below this is a list of all symbols used on the
maps in all the atlases in this series.
The legend on the right, below, is an example of a
legend used in the physical atlas.

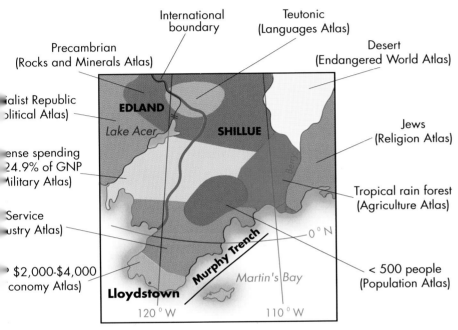

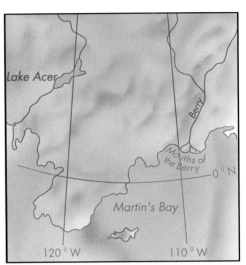

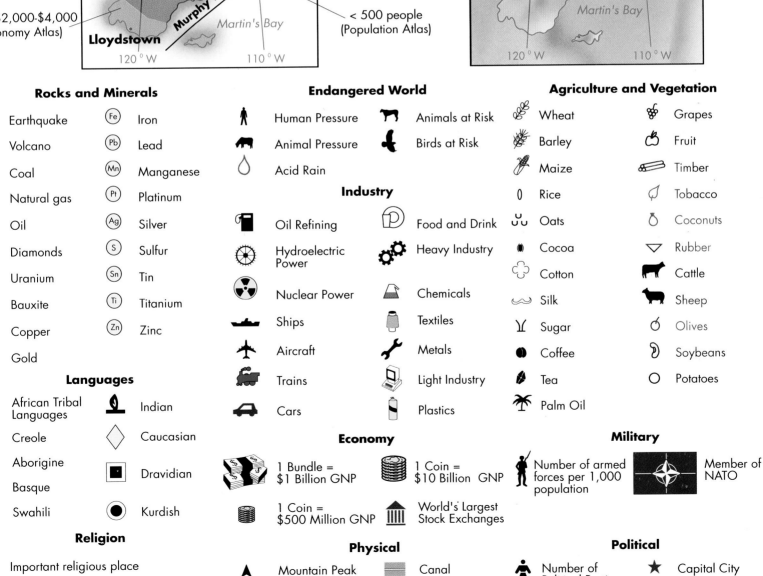

Rocks and Minerals

Earthquake		(Fe)	Iron
Volcano		(Pb)	Lead
Coal		(Mn)	Manganese
Natural gas		(Pt)	Platinum
Oil		(Ag)	Silver
Diamonds		(S)	Sulfur
Uranium		(Sn)	Tin
Bauxite		(Ti)	Titanium
Copper		(Zn)	Zinc
Gold			

Languages

African Tribal Languages	♦	Indian
Creole	◇	Caucasian
Aborigine	■	Dravidian
Basque		
Swahili	●	Kurdish

Religion

Important religious place

Endangered World

👤 Human Pressure	🐂 Animals at Risk
🐘 Animal Pressure	🦅 Birds at Risk
💧 Acid Rain	

Industry

Oil Refining	Food and Drink
Hydroelectric Power	Heavy Industry
Nuclear Power	Chemicals
Ships	Textiles
Aircraft	Metals
Trains	Light Industry
Cars	Plastics

Economy

1 Bundle = $1 Billion GNP	1 Coin = $10 Billion GNP
1 Coin = $500 Million GNP	World's Largest Stock Exchanges

Physical

▲ Mountain Peak		Canal

Agriculture and Vegetation

Wheat		Grapes
Barley		Fruit
Maize		Timber
Rice		Tobacco
Oats		Coconuts
Cocoa		Rubber
Cotton		Cattle
Silk		Sheep
Sugar		Olives
Coffee		Soybeans
Tea		Potatoes
Palm Oil		

Military

Number of armed forces per 1,000 population		Member of NATO

Political

Number of Political Parties	★	Capital City

World Physical

This page is a physical map of the world. It indicates where the major physical features — such as mountain ranges, plains, deserts, lakes, and rivers — are in the world. As the world is very large, the map has to be drawn at a very small scale in order to fit onto a page. This map is drawn at a scale so that 1 inch on the map, at the equator, equals 1,840 miles on the ground.

30°E 60°E 90°E 120°E 150°E
Severnaya Zemlya
New Siberian Islands
Novaya Zemlya
75°N
Arctic Circle
Scandinavia
West Siberian Plain
Siberia
60°N
Ural Mountains
Yenisey
Lena
Stanovoy Range
Sea of Okhotsk
Kamchatka Peninsula
North European Plain
Altai
Lake Baikal
Amur
Sakhalin
Carpathians
Volga
Aral Sea
Gobi
45°N
Danube
Caspian Sea
Lake Balkhash
Huang
Sea of Japan
Hokkaido
Black Sea
Caucasus Mtns
Balkan Peninsula
Tian Shan
Taklimakan Desert
Honshu
Anatolia
Tigris
Euphrates
Kunlun Mtns
Plateau of Tibet
Yangtze
East China Sea
30°N
PACIFIC
Mediterranean Sea
Nile
Red Sea
Persian Gulf
Himalaya
Indus
Ganges
▲Mount Everest 29,028 ft.
Tropic of Cancer
OCEAN
ara
Arabian Peninsula
Deccan Plateau
Bay of Bengal
Mekong
Taiwan
Hainan
Arabian Sea
Philippines
15°N
Blue Nile
White Nile
Ethiopian Highlands
Sri Lanka
South China Sea
Micronesia
Congo
Congo Basin
Lake Victoria
▲Kilimanjaro 19,340 ft.
Seychelles
Sumatra
Borneo
Equator 0°
Lake Tanganyika
Java
New Guinea
Melanesia
Lake Nyasa
INDIAN
15°S
Zambezi
Mozambique Channel
Madagascar
OCEAN
Coral Sea
Tropic of Capricorn
Kalahari Desert
Great Victoria Desert
Darling
Great Dividing Range
New Zealand
30°S
Drakensberg
Tasman Sea
Cape of Good Hope
Tasmania
Mount Cook▲ 12,349 ft.
45°S
60°S
N
OCEAN
75°S
ntarctica
30°E 60°E 90°E 120°E 150°E

World Key Map

Africa, Northern 10-11

Algeria
Benin
Burkina Faso
Cameroon
Cape Verde
Central African Republic
Chad
Djibouti
Egypt
Ethiopia
Gambia
Ghana
Guinea
Guinea-Bissau
Ivory Coast
Liberia
Libya
Mali
Mauritania
Morocco
Niger
Nigeria
Senegal
Sierra Leone
Somalia
Sudan
Togo
Tunisia
Western Sahara

Africa, Southern 12-13

Angola
Botswana
Burundi
Comoros
Congo
Equatorial Guinea
Gabon
Kenya
Lesotho
Madagascar
Malawi
Mauritius
Mozambique
Namibia
Rwanda

São Tomé & Príncipe
Seychelles
South Africa
Swaziland
Tanzania
Uganda
Zaire
Zambia
Zimbabwe

America, Central 14-15

Antigua & Barbuda
Bahamas
Barbados
Belize
Costa Rica
Cuba
Dominica

Dominican Republic
El Salvador
Grenada
Guatemala
Haiti
Honduras
Jamaica

Mexico
Nicaragua
Panama
St Kitts - Nevis
St Lucia
St Vincent
Trinidad & Tobago

Canada 26-27

Canada

Commonwealth of Independent States 28-29

Armenia
Azerbaijan
Estonia
Georgia
Kazakhstan
Kirghizstan
Latvia
Lithuania
Moldova
Russian Federation

Tajikistan
Turkmenistan
Ukraine
Uzbekhistan

Europe 30-31

Albania
Bosnia & Herzegovina
Bulgaria
Croatia
Czechoslovakia
Finland
Greece
Hungary
Iceland
Norway

Poland
Romania
Slovenia
Sweden
Yugoslavia

Europe, Western 32-33

Andorra
Austria
Belgium
Denmark
France
Germany
Ireland
Italy
Liechtenstein
Luxembourg

Malta
Monaco
Netherlands
Portugal
San Marino
Spain
Switzerland
United Kingdom
Vatican City

America, South 16-17

Argentina
Bolivia
Brazil
Chile
Colombia
Ecuador
French Guiana

Guyana
Paraguay
Peru
Suriname
Uruguay
Venezuela

Antarctica 18-19

Antarctica

Asia, East 20-21

China
Japan
Korea, North
Korea, South
Mongolia
Taiwan

Asia, Southeast 22-23

Brunei
Burma
Cambodia
Indonesia
Laos
Malaysia
Philippines
Singapore
Thailand
Vietnam

Australasia 24-25

Australia
New Zealand
Papua New Guinea

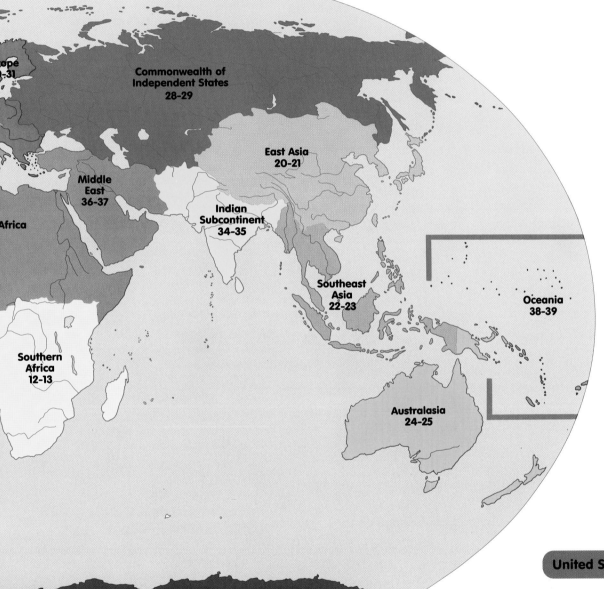

United States of America 40-41

United States of America

Indian Subcontinent 34-35

Afghanistan
Bangladesh
Bhutan
India
Maldives
Nepal
Pakistan
Sri Lanka

Middle East 36-37

Bahrain
Cyprus
Iran
Iraq
Israel
Jordan
Kuwait
Lebanon
Oman
Qatar

Saudi Arabia
Syria
Turkey
United Arab Emirates
Yemen

Oceania 38-39

Fiji
Kiribati
Nauru
Solomon Islands
Tonga
Tuvalu
Vanuatu
Western Samoa

This region, prosperous in ancient times, is now regaining some of its former economic strength with the discovery of rich reserves of oil and gas in some northern countries, allowing investment in modern industries. Some of the poorest nations are also to be found in this region.

Industrialization

Economic activity is usually divided into three sections:
Agriculture
Industry
Services
Industry includes mining, construction, manufacturing, and utilities such as electricity, gas, and water supply.

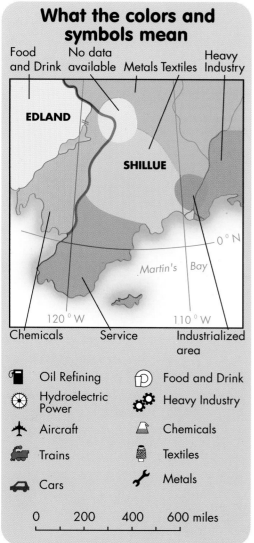

What the colors and symbols mean

| Food and Drink | No data available | Metals | Textiles | Heavy Industry |

EDLAND

SHILLUE

Martin's Bay

| Chemicals | Service | Industrialized area |

120°W   110°W

Symbol	Meaning	Symbol	Meaning
	Oil Refining		Food and Drink
	Hydroelectric Power		Heavy Industry
	Aircraft		Chemicals
	Trains		Textiles
	Cars		Metals

0   200   400   600 miles

Services include the wholesale and retail trade, restaurants, hotels, transportation, communications, financial services, and personal and social services.

A country is said to be industrialized when the proportion of the Gross Domestic Product (GDP) in the industrial sector reaches a high level. In addition there is almost invariably a large increase in the service sector to cope with the increase in industrialization.

An industrialized country generally has at least 25% of its GDP in industry. A substantial proportion of industrial output should be in manufacturing, and at least 10% of the population should be employed in industry.

Developed countries with one-sixt of the world's population produce three-quarters of the world's industrial output.

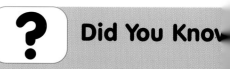

? Did You Know

★ The word *industry* also means steady and continuous work.

★ Machines and robots in factories can now do the work that people used to do.

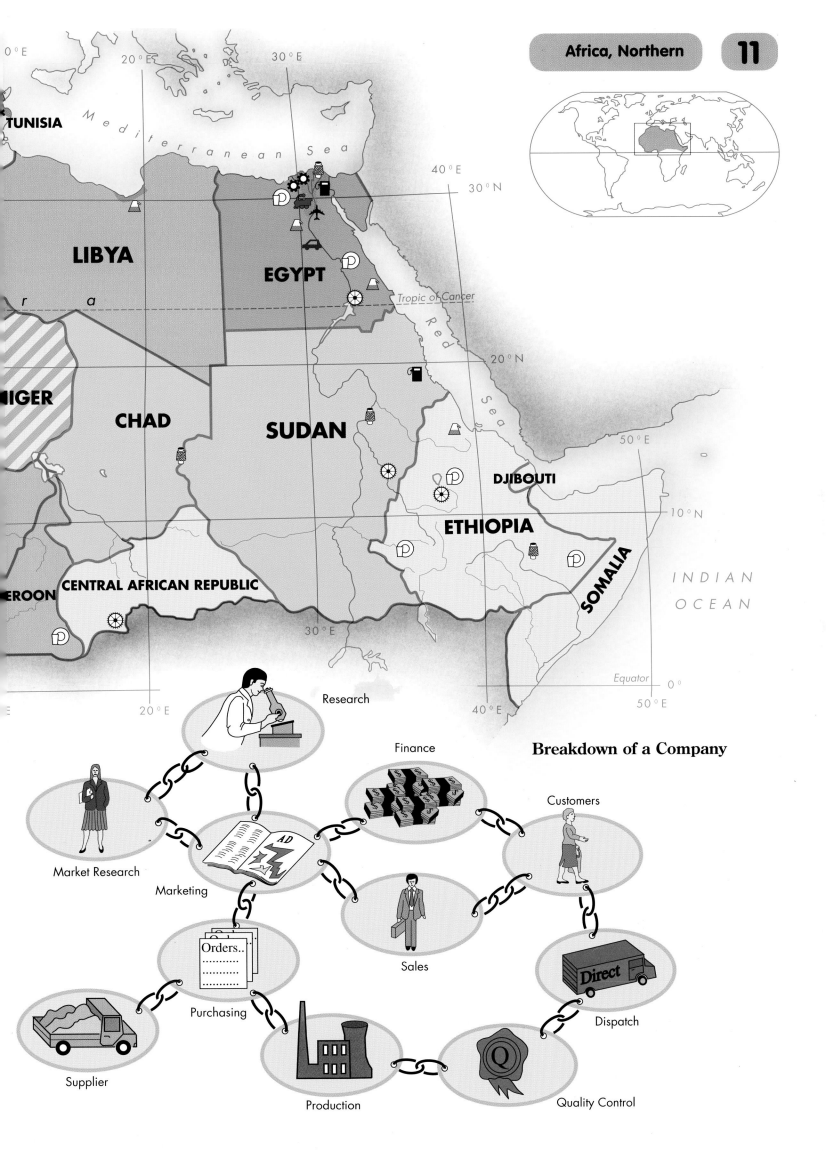

TUNISIA

Mediterranean Sea

LIBYA

EGYPT

30°N

Tropic of Cancer

IGER

CHAD

SUDAN

Red Sea

20°N

CENTRAL AFRICAN REPUBLIC

EROON

DJIBOUTI

ETHIOPIA

SOMALIA

INDIAN OCEAN

10°N

Equator 0°

20°E 30°E 40°E 50°E

Breakdown of a Company

Research

Finance

Customers

Market Research

Marketing

Sales

Orders..

Purchasing

Dispatch

Supplier

Production

Quality Control

This is an economically diverse area with vast mineral resources in the Congo and in the south but very little real industrialization, except in South Africa.

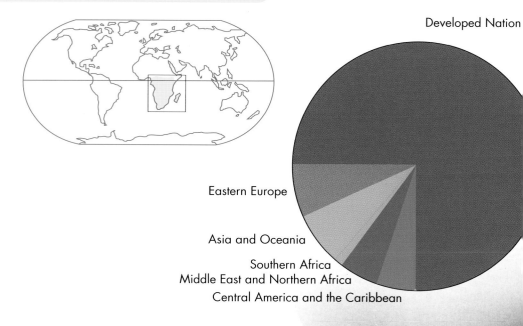

Developed Nation

Eastern Europe

Asia and Oceania

Southern Africa
Middle East and Northern Africa
Central America and the Caribbean

Industrial Growth Rates

Developed countries have already established their industrial base, so their growth rates are much lower than newly industrialized states — particularly those in Asia, such as China, South Korea, Singapore, Taiwan, and Hong Kong.

Sub-Saharan Africa, with its small markets and poorly developed infrastructure, lags behind in industrial growth.

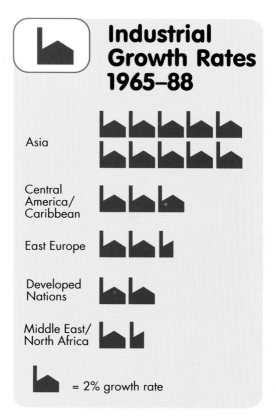

Industrial Growth Rates 1965–88

Asia

Central America/ Caribbean

East Europe

Developed Nations

Middle East/ North Africa

= 2% growth rate

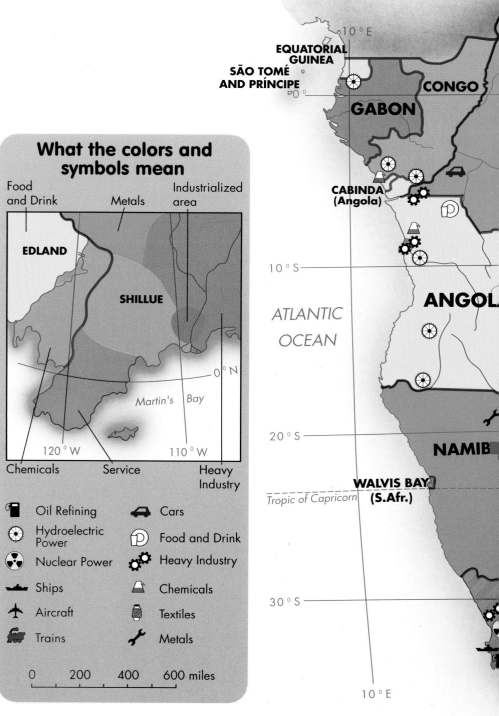

What the colors and symbols mean

Food and Drink

Metals

Industrialized area

EDLAND

SHILLUE

Martin's Bay

Chemicals

Service

Heavy Industry

Symbol	Meaning	Symbol	Meaning
	Oil Refining		Cars
	Hydroelectric Power		Food and Drink
	Nuclear Power		Heavy Industry
	Ships		Chemicals
	Aircraft		Textiles
	Trains		Metals

0   200   400   600 miles

10° E

EQUATORIAL GUINEA

SÃO TOMÉ AND PRÍNCIPE

CONGO

GABON

CABINDA (Angola)

10° S

ANGOL

ATLANTIC OCEAN

0° N

20° S

NAMIB

WALVIS BAY (S.Afr.)

Tropic of Capricorn

30° S

10° E

men at Work

work women do in child
ring, child rearing, and
ntaining a home is seldom
gnized as "work," nor is the
aid agricultural labor provided
women in many underdeveloped
tries. Women's work is
erally either ignored or under-
rded in statistics, as women are
considered economically active
ey "produce significant amounts
arketable goods or visible
me."

ever, there are wide variations
e work patterns of women in
different countries, due to cultural
and socioeconomic differences.
The lowest rates of participation are
found in the Islamic countries of
North Africa and West Asia.
In Bangladesh and Pakistan, in
particular, less than 10% of women
are in the work force at any time.
The highest general level is found
in the Eastern European countries,
where apparently more than 70% of
women between the ages of 18 and
60 participate in the work force
however, directly comparable
figures are not available.

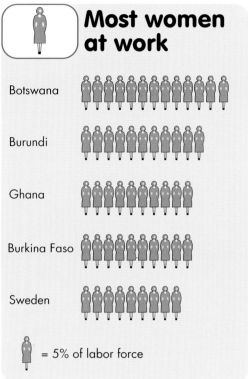

Most women at work

Botswana

Burundi

Ghana

Burkina Faso

Sweden

= 5% of labor force

Trade

Trade is an important way in which
countries relate to one another.

In addition, world trade is very
closely linked to the national
economic structure of most
countries. Some countries are more
vulnerable than others. Generally
countries with a high concentration
of exports rely on just a few
commodities for their export
earnings. These countries
invariably export primary products,
such as agricultural goods or
minerals. Countries with a low
export concentration usually export
a wide range of goods and are
generally more industrialized.

These countries are generally
less dependent on trade to
keep their economies stable.
When a country depends on just a
few items, it is potentially subject to
price fluctuations and slumps.
The economy of the country is
therefore very fragile. One of the
ways of overcoming this has been
to form cartels, or groups of
producers, who attempt to control
the level of production of the item
and the trade in order to stabilize
the price and maximize the return.

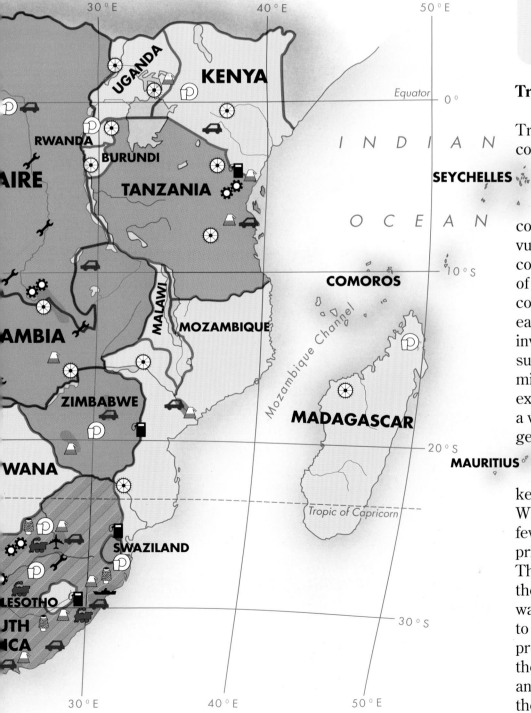

Numerous small countries dependent on tourism and agriculture are to be found in this area. The outstanding exception is oil-rich Mexico, which is developing and industrializing rapidly.

Aircraft Industry

Very few aircraft are mass produced, and only a few companies manufacture airplanes, but there are thousands of factories that supply aircraft parts to assembly plants. Suppliers specialize in making such components as fasteners, landing gear, or instruments, while others build the larger parts of aircraft — the wings, the fuselage, and the tail.

Designers and engineers begin to plan a plane long before it is ready for production. Transport and other large planes may take up to 10 years of planning. Every component must be as reliable as possible, and everything has to be as light in weight as it can be. An airplane cannot stop in midair if something goes wrong. So engineers carefully test and check all the metal, wood, and plastics that go into a new plane. They use a wind tunnel to test the effects of airflows over the model at different speeds.

Amazing — But True

★ The world's first jumbo jet to go into service was the Boeing 747, which could carry nearly 500 passengers. Now these planes carry fewer passengers but can travel a third of the world without refueling.

★ The fastest planes in the world have rocket engines.

? Did You Know

★ Concorde is a supersonic plane. Supersonic means that it can travel faster than the speed of sound. Earlier planes were torn apart when they reached this speed.

★ The galaxy C5 is the largest aircraft in the world. It has 28 wheels and its nose opens up so that it can carry military vehicles like tanks.

Transport Planes

Transport planes usually carry expensive, lightweight goods, such as electrical equipment and machine parts. They also carry goods that must be delivered quickly, such as fresh flowers, fruit and vegetables. Some planes can be adapted to carry containers. Once transport planes carried mainly mail, but now cargo handling is a growing part of the business of airports.

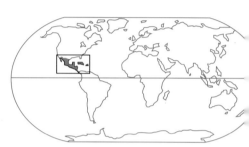

The Boeing 747 was the first jumbo jet.

Concorde is a supersonic jet built by France and the United Kingdom.

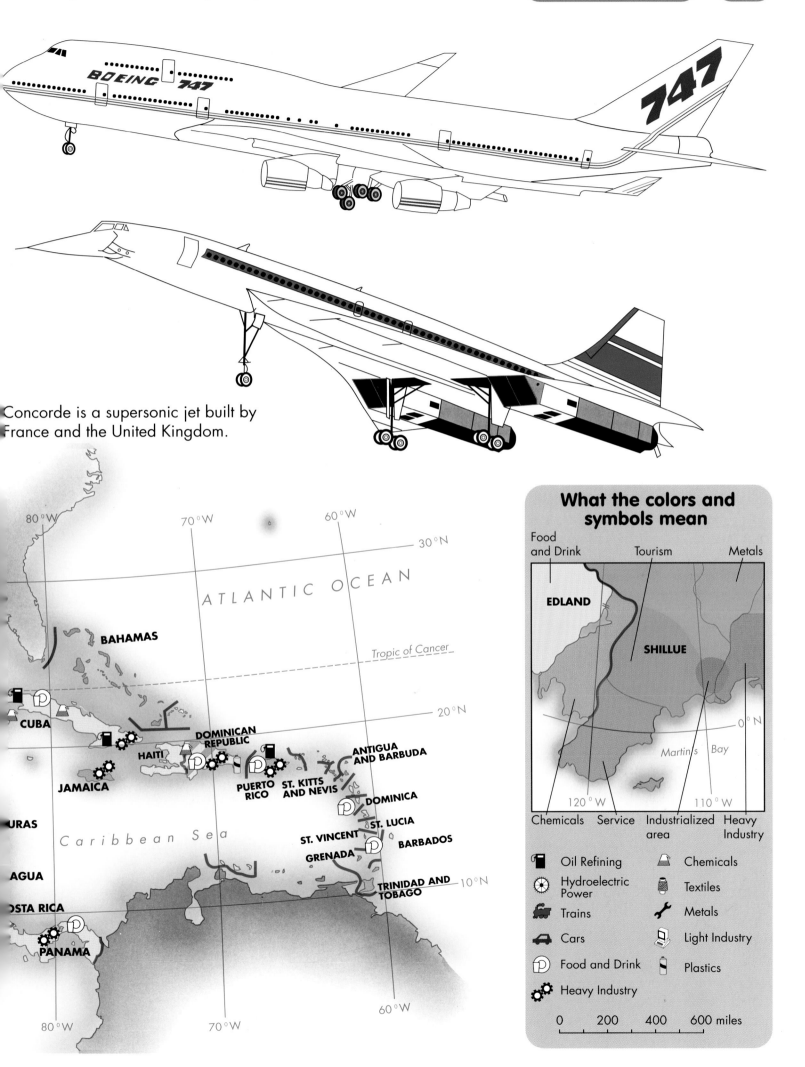

80°W   70°W   60°W

ATLANTIC OCEAN

30°N

20°N

Tropic of Cancer

BAHAMAS

CUBA

HAITI

DOMINICAN
REPUBLIC

JAMAICA

PUERTO
RICO

ST. KITTS
AND NEVIS

ANTIGUA
AND BARBUDA

DOMINICA

ST. LUCIA

URAS

Caribbean Sea

ST. VINCENT

GRENADA

BARBADOS

AGUA

TRINIDAD AND
TOBAGO   10°N

OSTA RICA

PANAMA

80°W   70°W   60°W

What the colors and symbols mean

Food
and Drink   Tourism   Metals

EDLAND

SHILLUE

30°N

20°N

0°N

Martin's   Bay

120°W   110°W

Chemicals   Service   Industrialized   Heavy
area   Industry

🛢 Oil Refining   ⬜ Chemicals

⚙ Hydroelectric   Textiles
Power

🚂 Trains   🔧 Metals

🚗 Cars   Light Industry

Ⓟ Food and Drink   Plastics

⚙ Heavy Industry

0   200   400   600 miles

Many nations in this vast and well-resourced continent are already well advanced along the road to industrialization. Brazil and Argentina in particular produce a wide range of top-quality manufactured goods.

Manufacturing

Today manufacturing means the making of articles by machinery as well as by hand. The manufacturing industry includes automobiles, books, clothing, furniture, paper, and thousands of other products.

Manufacturing is important because when a factory hires labor it creates jobs outside as well as inside the factory. The employers of the factory have to be serviced with goods. So factories and manufacturing benefit the whole community. Manufacturing can be subdivided into heavy and light, or durable and nondurable goods. Food is a nondurable item, while durable items such as saucepans have a relatively long life.

Products can be consumer goods or producer goods. Retail stores, such as drug stores, sell consumer goods to millions of buyers, while producer goods are used to make other products: some examples are springs, bearings, and printing presses.

Manufacturing industries are best located where there are good natural resources — good transport, mild climate, good labor supply — so they are often near big cities.

Manufacturing usually depends on the raw materials available in a country, although certain countries — Japan in particular — developed substantial industry with fairly limited natural resources.

Textile and clothing industries prosper in developing countries because labor is generally cheap and these industries do not require advanced technology. A number of Asian countries have used these industries as a basis for their industrialization. So have some poorer European countries, such as Portugal and Greece.

Breakdown of Manufacturing

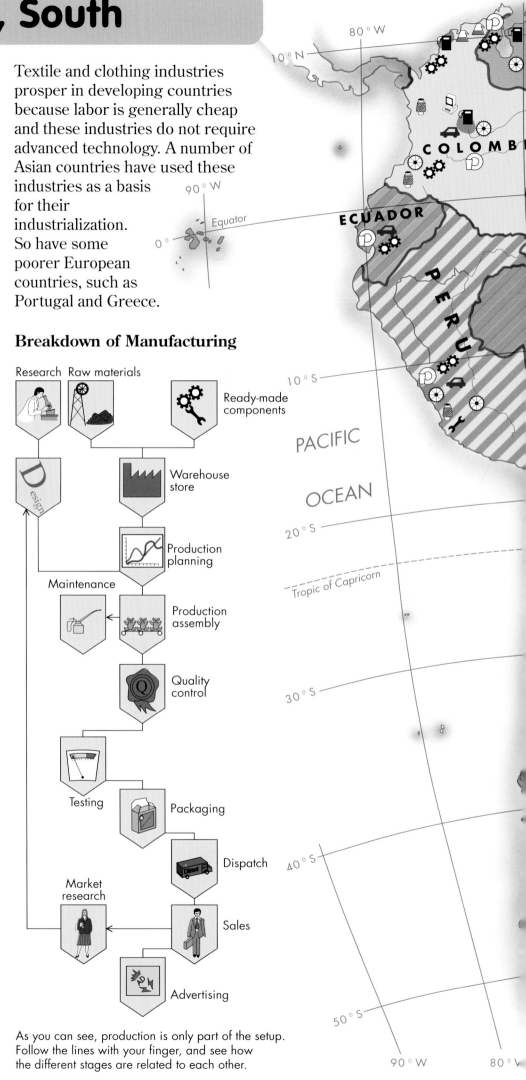

As you can see, production is only part of the setup. Follow the lines with your finger, and see how the different stages are related to each other.

Fewest women at work

Bangladesh

Pakistan

Algeria

Bahrain

Paraguay

= 5% of labor force

What the colors and symbols mean

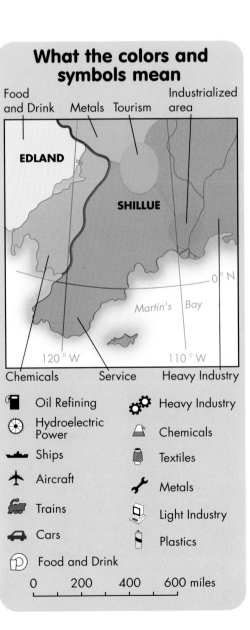

Food and Drink   Metals   Tourism   Industrialized area

EDLAND

SHILLUE

Martin's Bay

0° N

120° W   110° W

Chemicals   Service   Heavy Industry

🛢 Oil Refining		⚙ Heavy Industry	
✴ Hydroelectric Power		⛰ Chemicals	
🚢 Ships		🧵 Textiles	
✈ Aircraft		🔧 Metals	
🚂 Trains		💻 Light Industry	
🚗 Cars		Plastics	
Food and Drink			

0   200   400   600 miles

Amazing — But True

★ The greatest loss ever recorded was by the Argentine government petroleum company YPF (Yacimientos Petroliferos), which made a trading loss of $4.6 billion in 1983.

Equator

Tropic of Capricorn

ATLANTIC

OCEAN

Scotia Sea

VENEZUELA **GUYANA** **SURINAME** **FRENCH GUIANA**

B R A Z I L

B O L I V I A

PARAGUAY

URUGUAY

A R G E N T I N A

Fisheries are the main industry to be found in Antarctica, and these are increasingly subject to environmental controls. The largely unexplored mineral resources seem to be locked away for the forseeable future.

Tourism

The only commercial activity that takes place on the continent of Antarctica itself is tourism. Cruise liners have been operating tours, making brief stops at research bases, historical sites, and penguin rookeries.

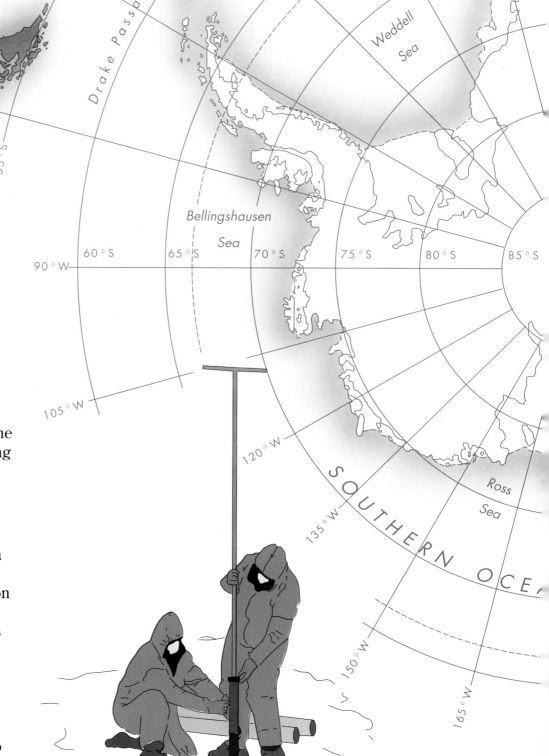

Scientific Research

There are over 30 year-round scientific stations in Antarctica. Geologists collect rock samples from the ice-free area. Biologists study marine and animal life. In addition, there is considerable scientific work on weather, earthquakes, and solar radiation. In the 1980s scientists made the important discovery that the ozone layer above Antarctica is becoming less concentrated.

Mineral Exploitation

Geologists believe that Antarctica contains considerable mineral wealth. Substantial deposits of iron ore, large reseves of coal, and numerous other minerals such as gold, titanium, tin, copper, cobalt, and uranium have been found. The harshness of the climate and terrain prevents profitable exploitation of these resources. However, it may prove possible to extract offshore oil and gas deposits in time.

Fishing

Large-scale trawling for fish has increased rapidly in the southern oceans, raising fears of future over-fishing in these waters. Krill catches in particular have been increasing rapidly as new catching and processing technologies have made these little shrimplike creatures an economically viable product.

Whaling

The southern ocean was the major whaling ground of the world for many years. The first whaling station was established in 1904 by a Norwegian company, and from there the industry grew. At its peak about 40,000 whales were killed every season. Whales were killed for their meat; for whale oil, used as fuel for lamps; for cooking; and for use in the manufacture of a variety of other commercial products, such as cosmetics, fertilizer, glue, medicines, and soap.

The International Whaling Commission was established in 1946 to regulate the industry, but it had limited success. In the 1970s fierce opposition to whaling from conservation groups arose, resulting in a temporary ban on commercial whaling in 1986.

Japan is one of the few countries to continue whaling, using a loophole in the agreement in order to catch whales for "scientific purposes."

Sealing

There were once vast populations of seals in the southern oceans, but these all but disappeared during the 19th and 20th centuries as a result of heavy exploitation for their fur and blubber.

The seal populations are now coming back to their former numbers, with the help of careful controls to protect them.

One of the three major industrial areas of the world, it is continuing to advance more rapidly than North America or Europe. Highly skilled and motivated labor forces in Japan, South Korea, and Taiwan enable these countries to produce a wide variety of products.

Chemical Industry

Chemicals play a vital role in the production of many manufactured goods — the chemical industry's major products include detergents, drugs, dyes, fertilizers, food preservatives, flavorings, glass, metal alloys, paper products, and synthetic fibers.

Most chemical products are basic chemicals that are used to manufacture other products. Sulfuric acid is the chief basic chemical in many countries; others include chlorine, nitrogen, and oxygen and alkalis such as lime, sodium hydroxide, and chemicals used in plastics.

Production is increasingly concentrated in multinational companies, which have plants in many countries. Most of them have extensive research and development departments. The growth of the chemical industry has brought with it many environmental and safety problems. For example, the use of huge amounts of pesticides has resulted in soil and water pollution. Harmful wastes that must be disposed of are often a by-product of the chemical industry, and some of the dumps used for storage of wastes have had harmful leaks. A number of accidents have occurred at chemical plants over the last few years.

! **Amazing — But True**

★ China makes three times as many bicycles as the USA. China is estimated to have 210 million bicycles.

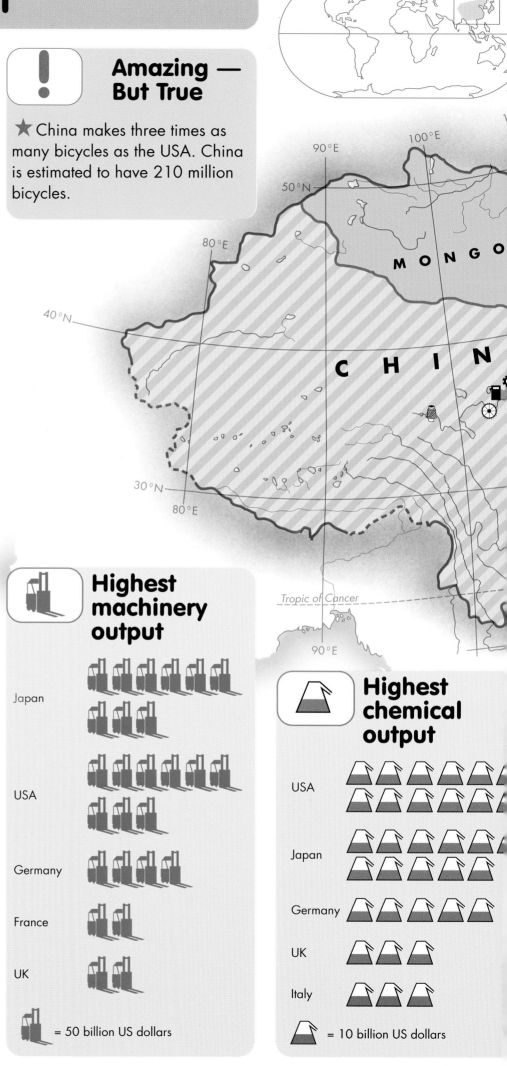

Highest machinery output

Japan
USA
Germany
France
UK

= 50 billion US dollars

Highest chemical output

USA
Japan
Germany
UK
Italy

= 10 billion US dollars

Newly Industrializing Countries

During the 1960s and 1970s a large number of underdeveloped countries were industrializing rapidly. They have become known as NICs (Newly Industrializing Countries).

The central core of NICs are Brazil, Mexico, South Korea, Hong Kong, Singapore, Taiwan, and Spain.
In addition, Greece, Portugal, and Yugoslavia can be included.
They are characterized by a fast growth in the level and share of industrial employment, an enlargement in the export market share of manufactured goods, and a reduction in the per capita income gap separating them from advanced countries.

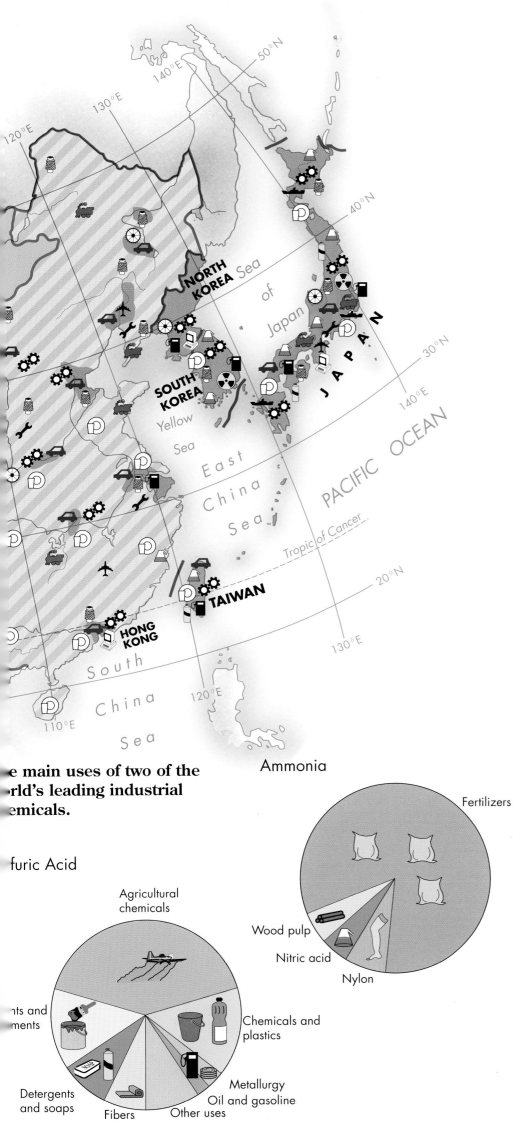

e main uses of two of the
rld's leading industrial
emicals.

Ammonia

furic Acid

Fertilizers

Agricultural chemicals

Wood pulp
Nitric acid
Nylon

nts and
ments

Chemicals and plastics

Detergents and soaps
Fibers
Metallurgy
Oil and gasoline
Other uses

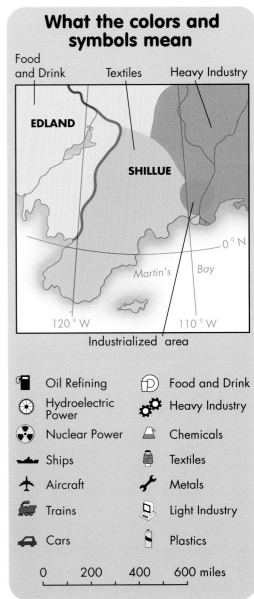

What the colors and symbols mean

Food and Drink — Textiles — Heavy Industry

EDLAND

SHILLUE

0°N

Martin's Bay

120°W   110°W

Industrialized area

Oil Refining	Food and Drink
Hydroelectric Power	Heavy Industry
Nuclear Power	Chemicals
Ships	Textiles
Aircraft	Metals
Trains	Light Industry
Cars	Plastics

0   200   400   600 miles

Asia, Southeast

Rich in agriculture and mineral resources with plentiful labor, this area is now rapidly industrializing, particularly in manufacturing industries such as textiles and clothing. This is reflected in the high growth rates in countries such as Indonesia, Malaysia, Singapore, and Thailand.

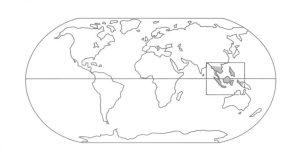

Two examples of different types of weave

Warp thre

Weft thre

Plain Weave

Textile Industry

The meaning of the word *textile* was originally "woven fabric," and many fabrics are still made by weaving; but today other products are considered textiles as well, such as knitted goods, laces, nets, braids, and felts.

Textile mills produce huge rolls of cotton, wool, nylon, and other fabrics in countless patterns and colors. The bulk of textile production goes to the garment industry for manufacture into ready-to-wear clothing; the next largest amount goes on household products such as sheets, towels, and blankets.

In the United States the textile industry manufactures about 25 billion square yards (21 billion square meters) of fabric a year.

Textiles are also used for a huge range of other products: flags, umbrellas, sails, book bindings, insulation. The automobile industry uses textiles for its car interiors, brake linings, and tires.

There are several stages in the textile industry — designing the fabric, making the yarn, making the fabric, and fabric finishing.

In the United States there are about 5,500 companies in this industry, operating over 7,000 plants. Many of them perform all stages of textile

production, but some specialize in one stage. A textile mill may produce cloth with yarn it buys from another supplier, then send on the cloth to a finishing firm.

This industry employs many people and provides jobs for skilled and unskilled workers; for this reason, it is a popular industry for newly developed countries with an abundant labor supply. Almost all countries have a textile industry. In developed countries the industry is highly mechanized, while in countries such as India and Pakistan, millions of workers weave cloth of cotton, silk, and other fibers in their homes.

Weaving with a hand loom is an old method being used by this woman from Indonesia.

Satin Weave

Highest textile output

Japan	
USA	
Italy	
Germany	
China	

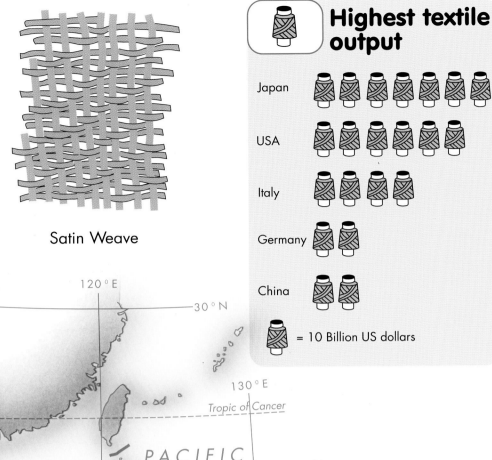

= 10 Billion US dollars

Some uses of textiles

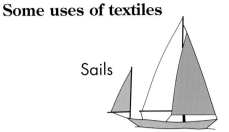

Sails

Bookbinding

Car interiors

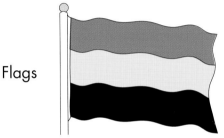

Flags

120°E

30°N

130°E

Tropic of Cancer

PACIFIC

OCEAN

20°N

South China Sea

PHILIPPINES

10°N

SIA

NEI

Celebes Sea

140°E

Equator 0°

a

INDONESIA

10°S

120°E

130°E

140°E

What the colors and symbols mean

Food and Drink   Industrialized area

EDLAND

SHILLUE

120°W   110°W   0°N

Martin's Bay

Chemicals   Heavy Industry

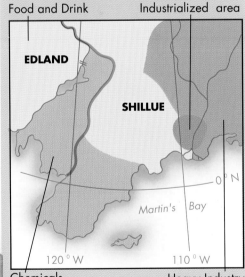

Oil Refining		Chemicals	
Hydroelectric Power		Textiles	
Cars		Metals	
Food and Drink		Plastics	
Heavy Industry			

0   200   400   600 miles

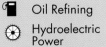

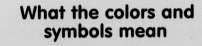

Substantial mineral and agricultural resources and a broad industrial base exist, particulary in Australia and New Zealand. However, a relatively small market and labor force has limited industrial development.

Food Industry

Agriculture and food processing is usually the industrial base for a developing country. This is the case for many African countries.
In developed countries, agriculture and food processing usually only account for about 20% of industry, except in countries that specialize in food production, such as New Zealand.

Highest food and agriculture output

USA	🛍️🛍️🛍️🛍️🛍️🛍️🛍️
Japan	🛍️🛍️🛍️🛍️🛍️
Germany	🛍️🛍️
France	🛍️🛍️🛍️
UK	🛍️🛍️

🛍️ = 20 billion US dollars

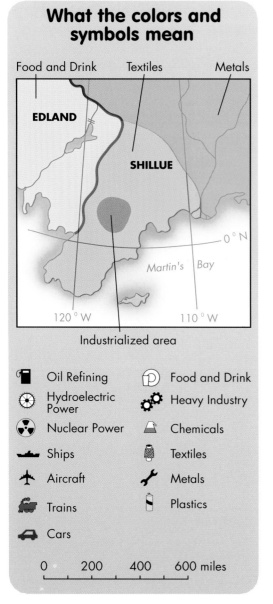

What the colors and symbols mean

Food and Drink   Textiles   Metals

EDLAND

SHILLUE

0°N

Martin's Bay

120°W   110°W

Industrialized area

🛢️ Oil Refining		🅿️ Food and Drink	
⊕ Hydroelectric Power		⚙️ Heavy Industry	
☢️ Nuclear Power		△ Chemicals	
🚢 Ships		🧵 Textiles	
✈️ Aircraft		🔧 Metals	
🚂 Trains		🔋 Plastics	
🚗 Cars			

0   200   400   600 miles

Examples of food packaging

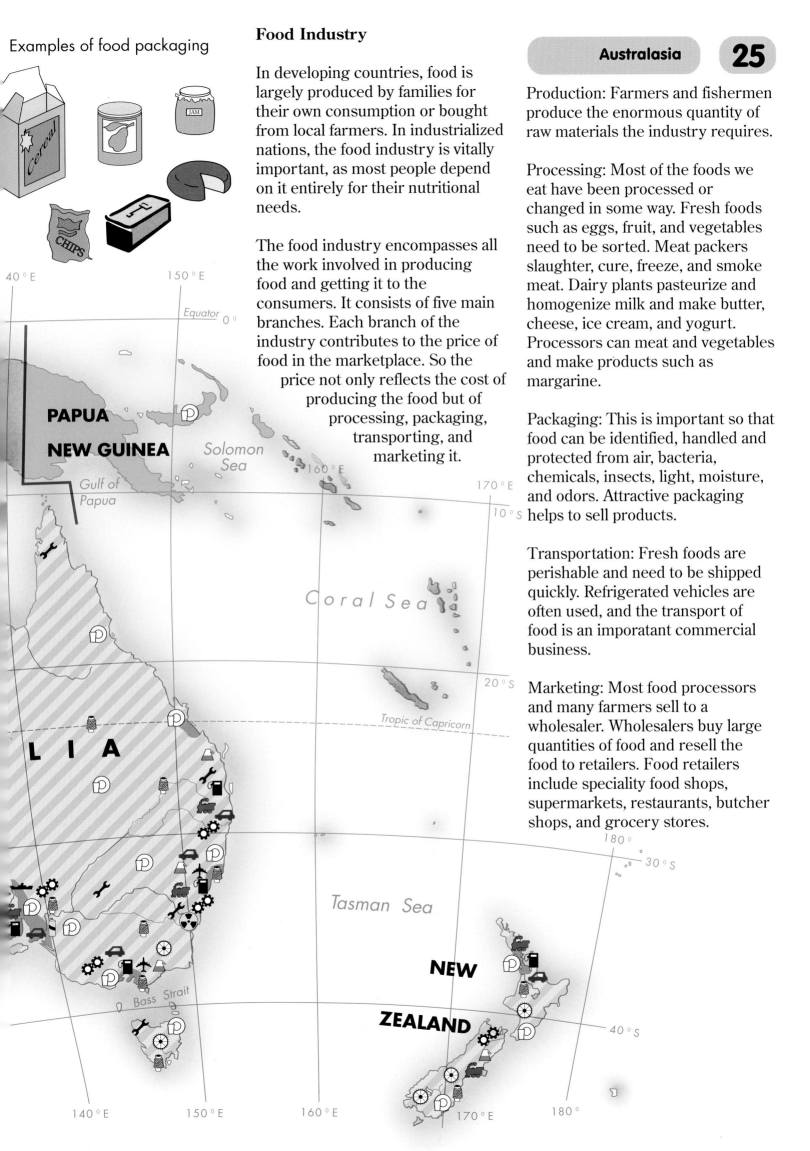

Food Industry

In developing countries, food is largely produced by families for their own consumption or bought from local farmers. In industrialized nations, the food industry is vitally important, as most people depend on it entirely for their nutritional needs.

The food industry encompasses all the work involved in producing food and getting it to the consumers. It consists of five main branches. Each branch of the industry contributes to the price of food in the marketplace. So the price not only reflects the cost of producing the food but of processing, packaging, transporting, and marketing it.

Production: Farmers and fishermen produce the enormous quantity of raw materials the industry requires.

Processing: Most of the foods we eat have been processed or changed in some way. Fresh foods such as eggs, fruit, and vegetables need to be sorted. Meat packers slaughter, cure, freeze, and smoke meat. Dairy plants pasteurize and homogenize milk and make butter, cheese, ice cream, and yogurt. Processors can meat and vegetables and make products such as margarine.

Packaging: This is important so that food can be identified, handled and protected from air, bacteria, chemicals, insects, light, moisture, and odors. Attractive packaging helps to sell products.

Transportation: Fresh foods are perishable and need to be shipped quickly. Refrigerated vehicles are often used, and the transport of food is an imporatat commercial business.

Marketing: Most food processors and many farmers sell to a wholesaler. Wholesalers buy large quantities of food and resell the food to retailers. Food retailers include speciality food shops, supermarkets, restaurants, butcher shops, and grocery stores.

Vast natural resources and highly developed industry with a wide range of products make Canada a strong economic area. Trade is very much linked to the American market.

Transportation of Trade

Most of the world's trade is carried by cargo ships. Ships carry wheat from Canada to Germany, machinery from Germany to Chile, and copper from Chile to Japan. Many different kinds of ships are used, but generally they fall into three categories:

Giant tankers and supertankers: These haul petroleum, soybean oil, and other liquids. These ships measure as much as 1,500 feet in length and 200 feet in width.

Dry bulk carriers: These haul grain, ore, sand, fertilizer, salt, or sugar — in fact, any dry bulk cargo. These ships may carry more than 100,000 short tons (91,000 metric tons) at a time.

General cargo ships: These transport anything from airplane engines to clothing. They may be refrigerator ships designed to transport fresh fruit, meat, or vegetables. Container ships are an important development because they eliminate the need for the hatches, holds, and derricks of the traditional cargo ship. The hull of a container ship is an enormous warehouse divided into cells by vertical guide rails. The cells are designed to hold prepackaged units called containers — a standard aluminum box about 20 feet long and 8 feet wide. They can be loaded and unloaded quickly, there is little chance of danger of damage to the cargo, and they can be transferred directly to trucks or railcars.

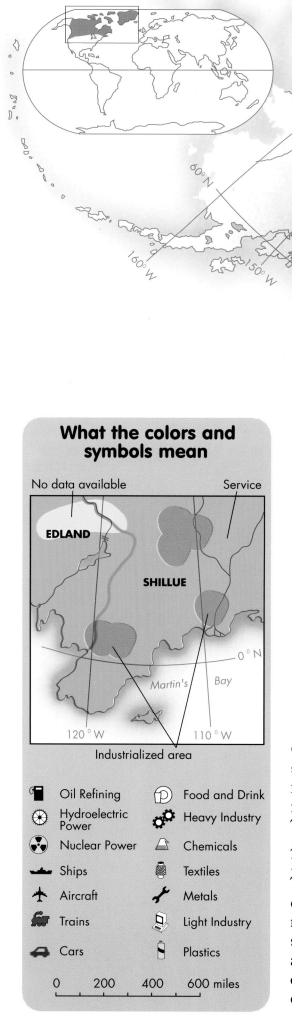

What the colors and symbols mean

No data available — EDLAND

SHILLUE

Service

Martin's Bay

0° N

120° W   110° W

Industrialized area

🔲 Oil Refining
⊛ Hydroelectric Power
☢ Nuclear Power
🚢 Ships
✈ Aircraft
🚂 Trains
🚗 Cars

ⓟ Food and Drink
⚙ Heavy Industry
△ Chemicals
🧵 Textiles
🔧 Metals
💻 Light Industry
🧴 Plastics

0   200   400   600 miles

Cargo ships offer two sorts of services. Liner services run on fixed schedules along certain tra[de] routes at published times and rat[es]. They usually carry general cargo. A round trip from the USA to Europe usually takes about 21 da[ys]. Tramp ships, however, do not sa[il] on regular trade routes or on regular schedules. They wander sea lanes and can be hired to hau[l] anything anywhere. Small shippi[ng] companies and private individual[s] operate the tramp ships.

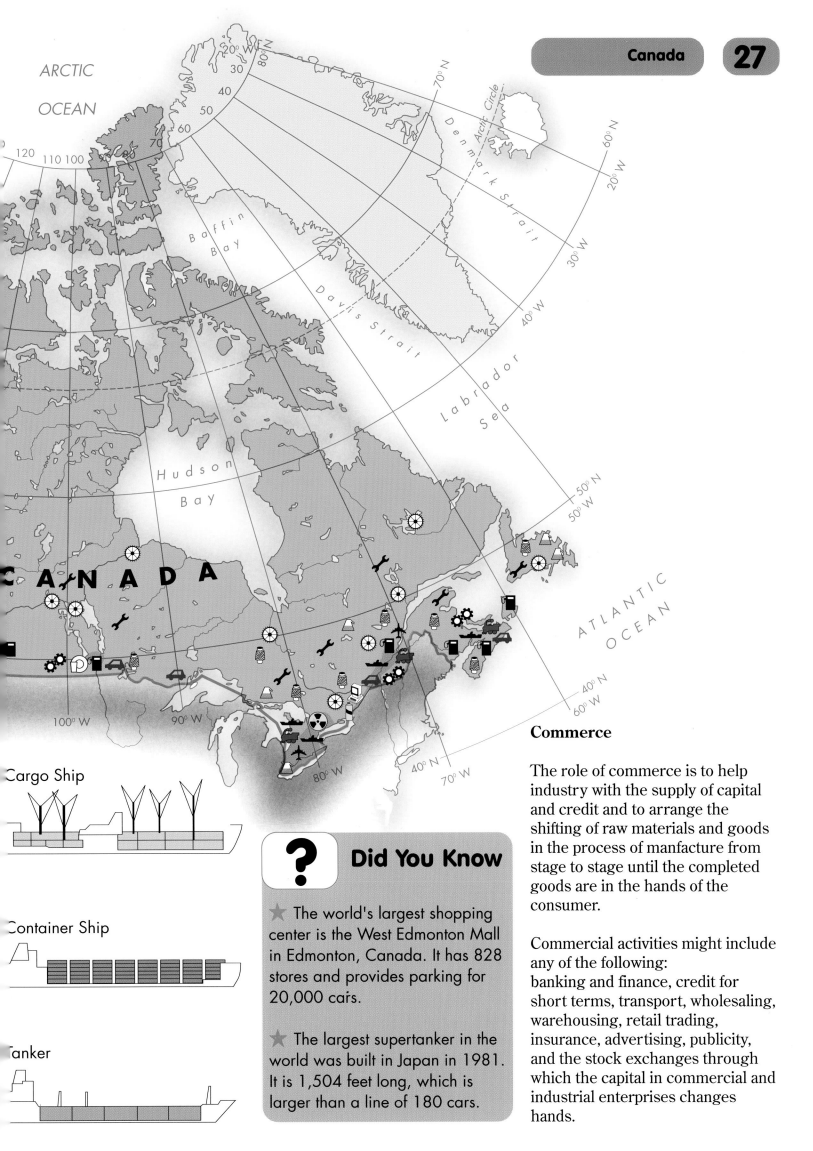

ARCTIC
OCEAN

Baffin
Bay

Denmark Strait

Arctic Circle

Davis Strait

Labrador
Sea

Hudson
Bay

C A N A D A

ATLANTIC
OCEAN

Commerce

The role of commerce is to help industry with the supply of capital and credit and to arrange the shifting of raw materials and goods in the process of manfacture from stage to stage until the completed goods are in the hands of the consumer.

Commercial activities might include any of the following: banking and finance, credit for short terms, transport, wholesaling, warehousing, retail trading, insurance, advertising, publicity, and the stock exchanges through which the capital in commercial and industrial enterprises changes hands.

Cargo Ship

Container Ship

Tanker

? Did You Know

★ The world's largest shopping center is the West Edmonton Mall in Edmonton, Canada. It has 828 stores and provides parking for 20,000 cars.

★ The largest supertanker in the world was built in Japan in 1981. It is 1,504 feet long, which is larger than a line of 180 cars.

Mining, steel, and other heavy industries predominate in this leading industrial area. However, problems with state planning and policies, low productivity, energy shortages, and a lack of skilled labor have severely handicapped the economies.

Railway Industry

Railways are an important means of transport — some trains carry passengers, while others haul freight — but almost every country has at least one railroad.

In most countries railroads are government owned and controlled.

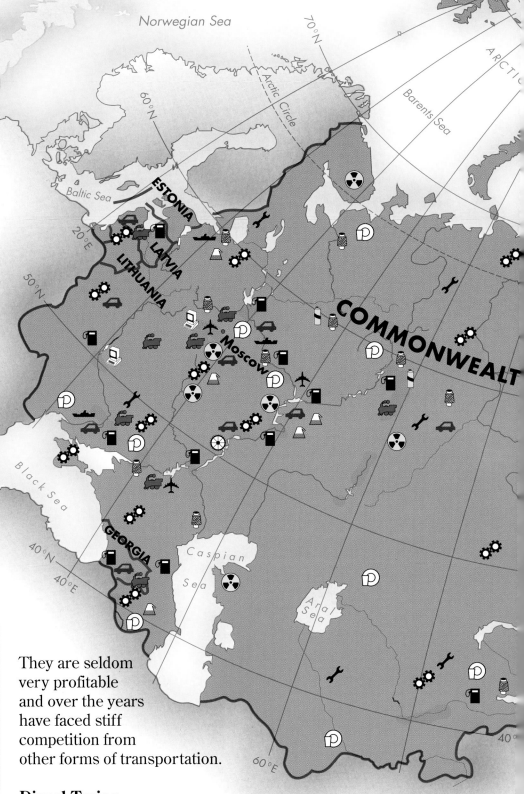

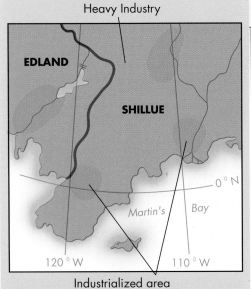

What the colors and symbols mean

🛢	Oil Refining	⚙	Heavy Industry
☢	Nuclear Power	△	Chemicals
⛴	Ships	🧵	Textiles
✈	Aircraft	🔧	Metals
🚂	Trains	📦	Light Industry
🚗	Cars	🏭	Plastics
Ⓟ	Food and Drink		

0   200   400   600 miles

They are seldom very profitable and over the years have faced stiff competition from other forms of transportation.

Diesel Trains

Diesel engines use diesel fuel, an oil derivative, to generate power. They are in effect mobile power plants, and because of this they have the great advantage of being able to operate on any rail lines that exist. They are relatively effecient and are able to make long runs without refueling or stopping.

TGV

The fastest passenger train in the world operates in France. Known the TGV (train à grande vitesse), it can travel at speeds of up to 18 miles per hour (300 kph). It offer an efficient service between Pari Lyon, and other French cities.

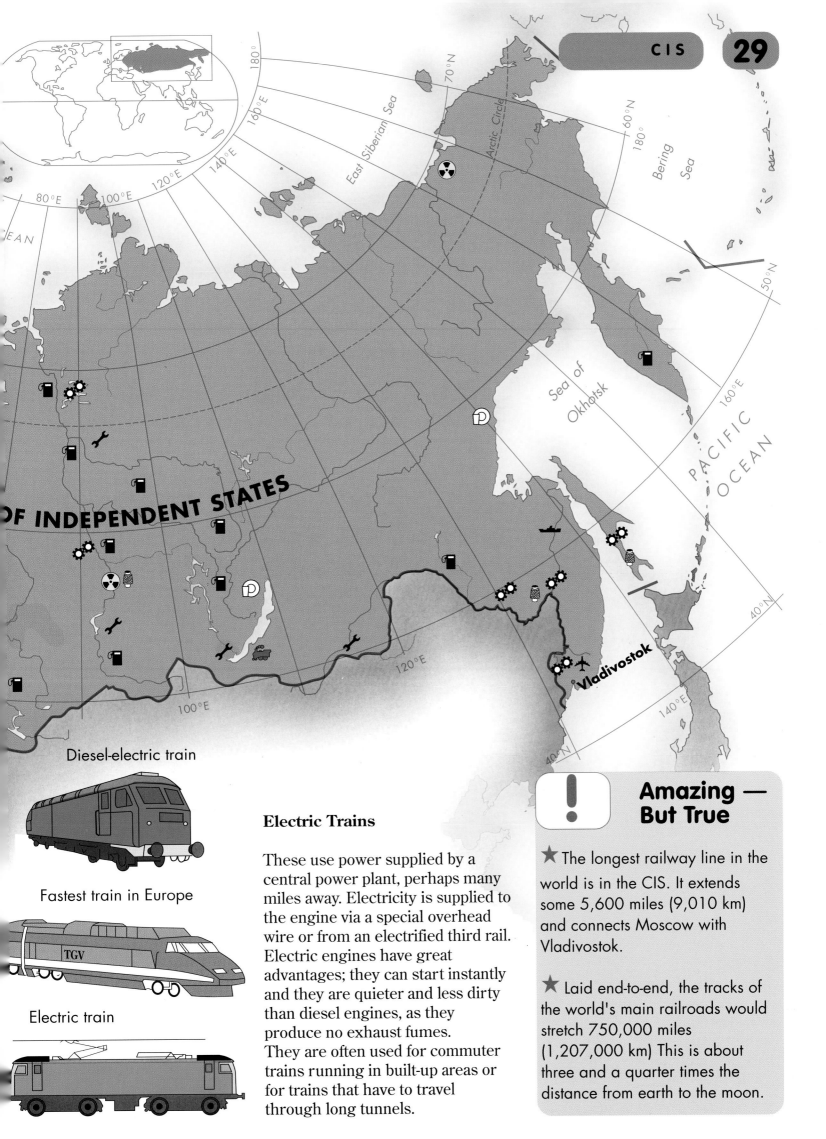

180°
70°N
160°E
East Siberian Sea
Arctic Circle
60°N
180°
Bering Sea
140°E
50°N
120°E
100°E
80°E
OCEAN
Sea of Okhotsk
160°E
PACIFIC OCEAN
OF INDEPENDENT STATES
120°E
40°N
100°E
40°N
140°E

Vladivostok

Diesel-electric train

Fastest train in Europe

TGV

Electric train

Electric Trains

These use power supplied by a central power plant, perhaps many miles away. Electricity is supplied to the engine via a special overhead wire or from an electrified third rail. Electric engines have great advantages; they can start instantly and they are quieter and less dirty than diesel engines, as they produce no exhaust fumes. They are often used for commuter trains running in built-up areas or for trains that have to travel through long tunnels.

! Amazing — But True

★ The longest railway line in the world is in the CIS. It extends some 5,600 miles (9,010 km) and connects Moscow with Vladivostok.

★ Laid end-to-end, the tracks of the world's main railroads would stretch 750,000 miles (1,207,000 km) This is about three and a quarter times the distance from earth to the moon.

Europe's substantial natural resources have been exploited over a considerable time period and enabled it to become the center of the first Industrial Revolution. Europe maintains its position as one of the three major industrial centers of the world, with a comprehensive range of industries.

Tourism

Tourism has become a profitable and highly competitive business as a result of growing wealth and better means of transport. Western Europe, North America, Japan, and Australia account for the majority of tourists. Europe is the destination of 85% of all tourists. Except for a few places, tourism is statistically insignificant in the Third World countries and in formerly Communist countries, despite their governments' need for foreign currency.

Many developing countries look upon tourism as a way of earning foreign currency and helping balance the outflow of capital on other goods while creating jobs. In practice the benefits may not always live up to expectations, and the earnings often fall into the hands of foreign airlines or hotel management companies. In addition, the demands of wealthy tourists may put an undue strain on already scarce resources.

Tourist business is dominated by the developed countries. 80% of spending is done by them, and nearly three-quarters of receipts fall into their hands. Scandinavians, Swiss, Austrians, and the Dutch are the highest spenders per capita, but in the 1980s the Japanese have become an increasingly powerful tourist force.

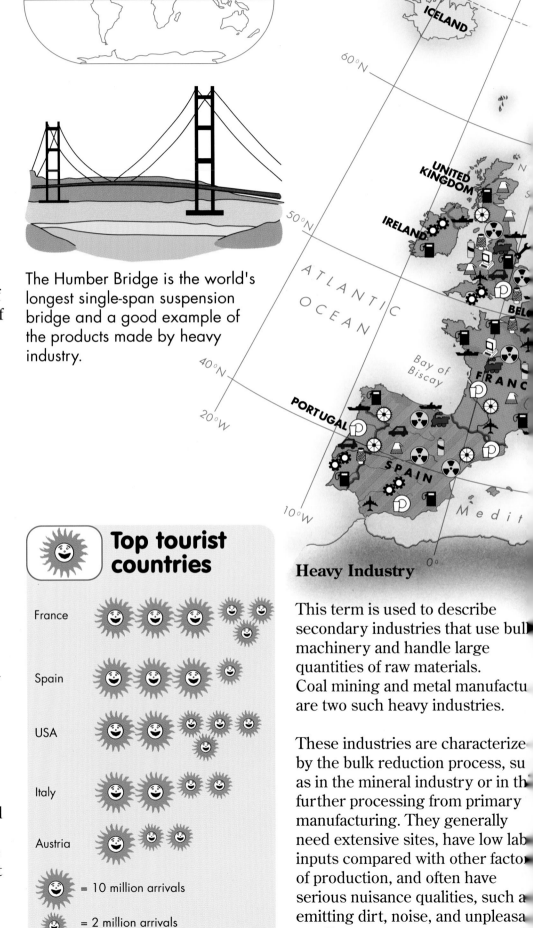

The Humber Bridge is the world's longest single-span suspension bridge and a good example of the products made by heavy industry.

Top tourist countries

France	●●● ●● ● (3.5 suns)
Spain	●●● ●
USA	●● ●●● ●
Italy	● ●●
Austria	● ●●

☀ = 10 million arrivals

☀ = 2 million arrivals

Heavy Industry

This term is used to describe secondary industries that use bulky machinery and handle large quantities of raw materials. Coal mining and metal manufacturing are two such heavy industries.

These industries are characterized by the bulk reduction process, such as in the mineral industry or in the further processing from primary manufacturing. They generally need extensive sites, have low labor inputs compared with other factors of production, and often have serious nuisance qualities, such as emitting dirt, noise, and unpleasant smells.

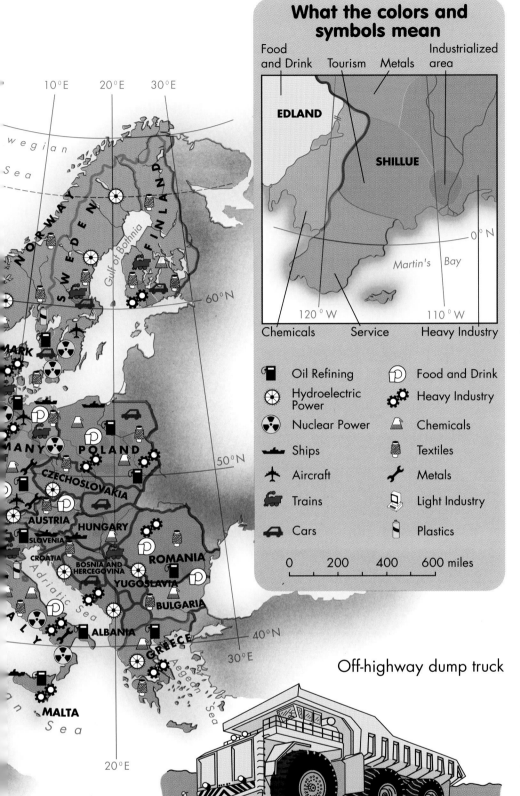

What the colors and symbols mean

Food and Drink · Tourism · Metals · Industrialized area

EDLAND

SHILLUE

Martin's Bay

Chemicals · Service · Heavy Industry

Oil Refining		Food and Drink	
Hydroelectric Power		Heavy Industry	
Nuclear Power		Chemicals	
Ships		Textiles	
Aircraft		Metals	
Trains		Light Industry	
Cars		Plastics	

0   200   400   600 miles

Multinational Corporations

Multinationals or transnationals are large companies that invest in two or more countries. These big firms have often been in the forefront of capitalist expansion and foreign investment, and they are often influential agents in terms of the world economy. At the end of the Second World War and during the following 20 years, US multinationals were by far the most influential. Since then Japanese and European multinationals have begun to challenge this dominance. The figures below show that the world's largest industrial firms are still largely US-based, but there has been a decline in the number of companies based in the USA.

$ Largest industrial companies

Sumitomo (Japan)	$161,040,000,000
C. Itoh (Japan)	$154,488,000,000
Mitsui & Co (Japan)	$152,738,000,000
General Motors (USA)	$143,142,000,000
Marubeni (Japan)	$137,300,000,000
Mitsubishi (Japan)	$125,004,000,000
Nissho Iwai (Japan)	$113,218,000,000
Ford Motor (USA)	$108,424,000,000
Exxon Corp (USA)	$108,346,000,000
Royal Dutch/Shell (Netherlands/UK)	$88,006,000,000

In order of sales

Off-highway dump truck

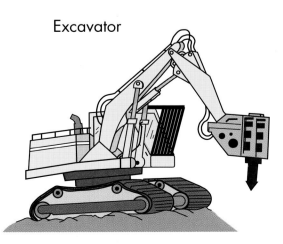

h technology is required for vy industry, such as the chinery and transport industries, so these tend to be stronger in eloped countries or newly ustrialized nations such as gapore, South Korea, and Brazil. he big economies of Japan, the ﾑ, Germany, France, Italy, and UK, machinery and transport erally account for a third or e of industrial output.

Excavator

! Amazing — But True

★ The largest off-highway dump truck in the world measures 67 feet long, which is as long as a line of eight cars, and can carry 350 tons.

Western Europe is the core of European economic strength and industrial power, with highly developed service industries of all kinds.

Shipbuilding Industry

People have been building ships since early times. Once, wood was the chief building material used, but during the 19th century a great change came over the industry when iron hulls were introduced. Later, steel became the main material of construction. Shipbuilding tended to be centered where raw materials (coal and iron) were available. For a time Britain was the leading shipbuilding nation. Following a huge shipbuilding program during World War II, the United States became the leader in the industry for a brief time in the 1940s. Increased expenses for labor and construction, priced the products of the United States out of the market. Since then, Japan has been the unchallenged leader in the production of merchant vessels, with an estimated 46% market share. In addition, Sweden, Germany, Spain, and the UK are strong in shipbuilding today.

Most ships registered

Liberia

Panama

Japan

Greece

CIS

= 5 million tons

Queen Elizabeth II (QE2)

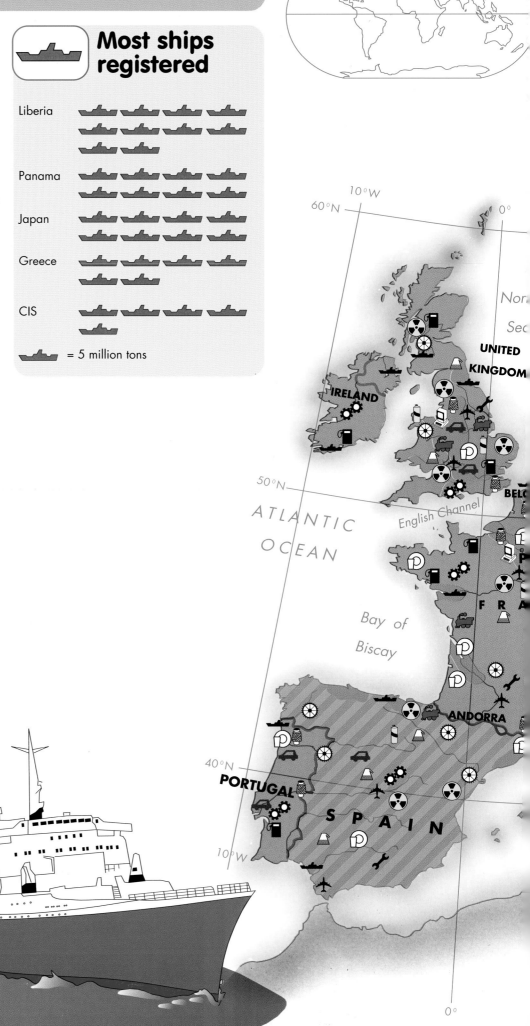

Light Industry

Secondary industries that are characterized by high-intensity use of space and produce goods of high value added or high value relative to their bulk and weight are known as light industries. Much of light industry consists of manufacturing, transforming small quantities of inputs with the aid of large amounts of (often unskilled) labor.

Industrial Efficiency

When countries develop, wages rise, and industry becomes more efficient in terms of labor input. In general, industrial output per capita is higher in more developed countries. Output per capita is also higher in major oil-producing countries, partly because of the nature of the industry and the wealth it produces.

More developed countries usually grow more slowly. Hence the strongest growth rates are to be found in rapidly industrializing countries, such as China and South Korea.

Industrial growth lags behind in African countries for a number of reasons. These include the poverty of the domestic and neighboring markets, poor infrastructure, shortage of capital for investment, and shortage of foreign exchange to import materials and technology.

What the colors and symbols mean

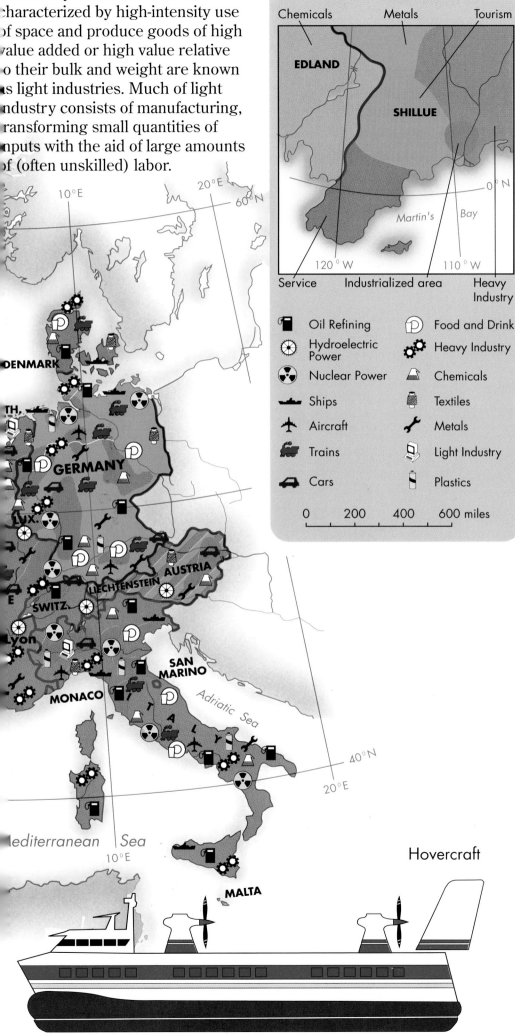

Symbol	Meaning	Symbol	Meaning
	Oil Refining		Food and Drink
	Hydroelectric Power		Heavy Industry
	Nuclear Power		Chemicals
	Ships		Textiles
	Aircraft		Metals
	Trains		Light Industry
	Cars		Plastics

0   200   400   600 miles

Hovercraft

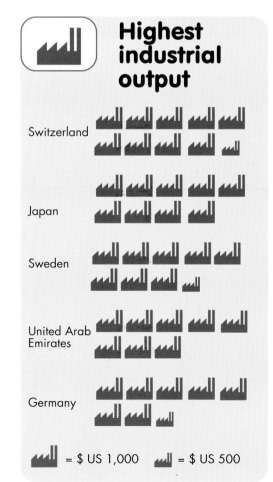

Highest industrial output

Switzerland	
Japan	
Sweden	
United Arab Emirates	
Germany	

= $ US 1,000   = $ US 500

Modernization programs and industrial progress have made India in particular a much stronger economy, with many skilled and highly trained workers. However, poverty, underemployment, and unemployment still plague this area.

The Labor Force

The labor force is made up of everyone who works, whether they are employed, self-employed, or unpaid workers in a family business, plus those who are out of work. The percentage of a country's population in its work force depends partly on its age structures. The proportion is lower in developing countries, where there are a lot of young people, and in developed countries, where there are a lot of older people. Other factors include the extent to which women work and the number of people who stay in school or who retire early.

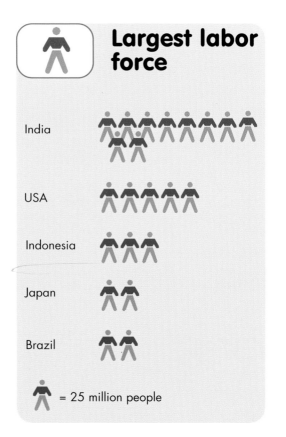

Largest labor force

India	👤👤👤👤👤👤👤👤👤
USA	👤👤👤👤👤
Indonesia	👤👤👤
Japan	👤👤
Brazil	👤👤

👤 = 25 million people

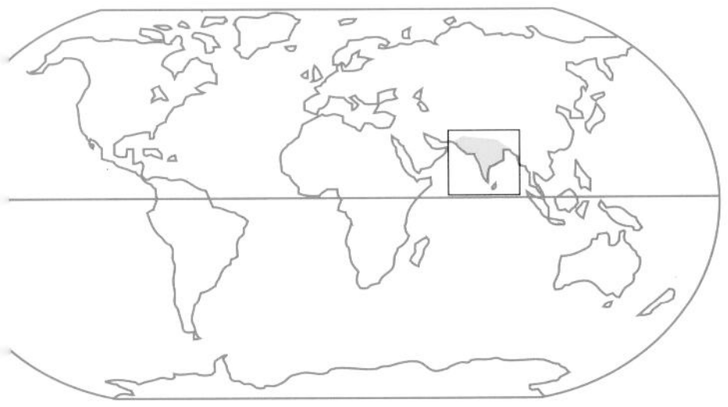

A large number of people are employed in the production of tea. This makes it a labor-intensive industry.

stribution of Labor Force

countries develop the labor e tends to move from agriculture luding forestry and fishing) industry and then move from ustry into services.

90°E   30°N

BHUTAN

BANGLADESH

Tropic of Cancer

20°N

? **Did You Know**

★ The world's largest employer is Indian Railways, with 1,617,613 employees in 1987–88.

B a y o f

B e n g a l

Andaman Sea

10°N

90°E

C E A N

What the colors and symbols mean

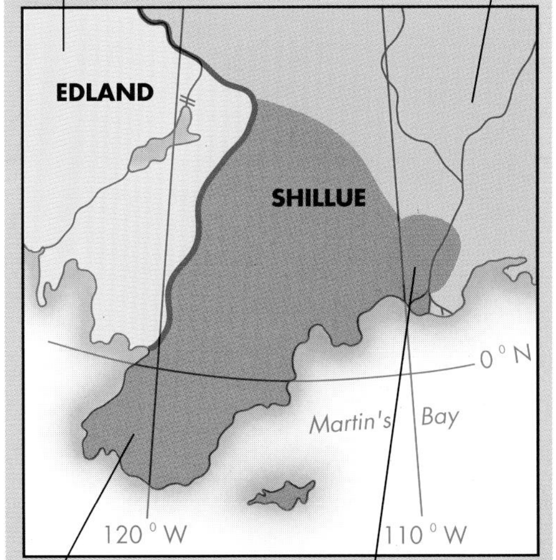

Food and Drink   Textiles

EDLAND

SHILLUE

0°N

Martin's   Bay

120°W   110°W

Service   Industrialized area

🛢	Oil Refining	Ⓟ	Food and Drink
⚙	Hydroelectric Power	⚙	Heavy Industry
☢	Nuclear Power	🔺	Chemicals
🚢	Ships	🧵	Textiles
✈	Aircraft	🔧	Metals
🚂	Trains	💻	Light Industry
🚗	Cars	🧴	Plastics

0   200   400   600 miles

The rich oil resources of the Middle East have been aggressively exploited in the last 40 years. Infrastructure has been developed, investment encouraged, and a start made in diversifying economies into new areas.

Petroleum Industry

The petroleum industry is one of the world's largest industries. It has four main branches: the production industry explores for oil and brings it to the surface; the transportation branch sends crude oil to refineries and delivers refined oil to its customers; the manufacturing branch processes crude oil into useful products; and the marketing branch sells and distributes petroleum to customers via service stations.

The petroleum industry plays a major role in the economies of a great number of nations and employs many people. It is a major buyer of iron, steel, and motor vehicles. In some oil-rich nations it provides most of the national income. It may even be a source of political power for oil producers because many other countries depend on them. Oil refineries range from small plants that process about 150 barrels of crude a day to giant complexes with a round-the-clock schedule that handles 600,000 barrels a day. The basic job is to convert crude petroleum into useful products, and the refineries separate the oil into various hydrocarbon groups or factions. These are then treated and converted to other substances.

The United States is one of the leading producers and refiners of petroleum. About 3 billion barrels of crude oil are produced by US wells annually. Only the CIS produces more.

Cartels

When a country depends on just a few items, it is potentially subject to price fluctuations and slumps. The economy of the country is therefore very fragile. One of the ways of overcoming this has been to form cartels, or groups of producers, who attempt to control the level of production of the item and the trade in order to stabilize the price and maximize the return.

The Organization of Petroleum Exporting Countries (OPEC)

The best known cartel is OPEC (Organization of Petroleum Exporting Countries). It was established in 1960. During the 1970s it controlled 65% of world petroleum exports, and prices rose tenfold in that period. Now OPEC members produce only 33% of the world's oil.

The products we can extract from oil

Butane

Bottled Gases — Petroleum gas

80°C
Cooler at the top

Petrol, plastics, chemicals — Gasoline

Aircraft fuel — Kerosene

Refining Tower

Diesel oil — Gas oil

Candles & lubricants — Waxes and lubricants

Crude oil is heated and turned to vapor. It enters the refining tower where it separates.

Ships & factories — Heavy fuel oils

Hotter at the bottom
350°C

Surfacing for roads & roofs — Bitumen

IRAN

60°E

30°N

BAHRAIN

QATAR

Gulf

Gulf of Oman

Tropic of Cancer

UNITED ARAB EMIRATES

60°E

OMAN

20°N

Arabian Sea

$ Cartels are effective when:

1. The demand elasticity for the product is low — in other words, there are no easy substitutes for it.

2. Stocks are low in consuming countries.

3. Cartel members have enough economic strength to survive loss of earnings longer than consuming countries are willing to do without the commodity.

4. The cartel is politically cohesive.

5. Cartel members control a major part of world production.

What the colors and symbols mean

Food and Drink

Tourism

EDLAND

SHILLUE

0° N

Martin's Bay

120° W

110° W

Chemicals   Service   Heavy Industry

Oil Refining   Heavy Industry

Hydroelectric Power   Chemicals

Aircraft   Textiles

Trains   Metals

Cars   Plastics

Food and Drink

0   200   400   600 miles

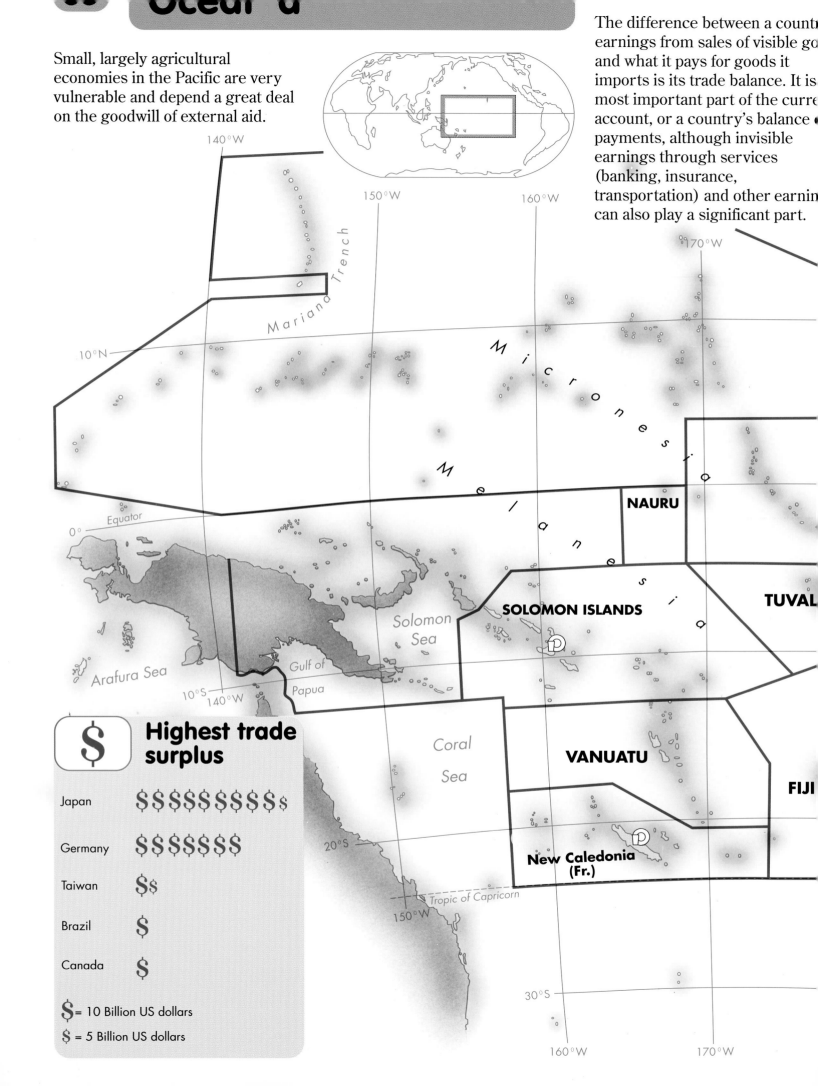

Small, largely agricultural economies in the Pacific are very vulnerable and depend a great deal on the goodwill of external aid.

The difference between a country earnings from sales of visible goods and what it pays for goods it imports is its trade balance. It is most important part of the current account, or a country's balance of payments, although invisible earnings through services (banking, insurance, transportation) and other earnings can also play a significant part.

140°W

150°W

160°W

170°W

Mariana Trench

10°N

Micronesia

Melanesia

NAURU

Equator

0°

SOLOMON ISLANDS

TUVAL

Solomon Sea

Arafura Sea

Gulf of

10°S 140°W

Papua

Coral Sea

VANUATU

FIJI

20°S

New Caledonia (Fr.)

Tropic of Capricorn

150°W

30°S

160°W

170°W

Highest trade surplus

Japan	$$$$$$$$$
Germany	$$$$$$$
Taiwan	$$
Brazil	$
Canada	$

$ = 10 Billion US dollars

$ = 5 Billion US dollars

Highest trade deficit

USA	$$$$$$$$$$ $$$$ $
UK	$$
Spain	$
France	$
India	$

$ = -10 Billion US dollars

$ = -5 Billion US dollars

Developing countries may be able to generate a trade surplus but find it is worn away by payments for invisibles or interest on their foreign debt. Countries such as Mexico are then obliged to run export surpluses, perhaps by restricting imports, to pay for their foreign debt.

What the colors and symbols mean

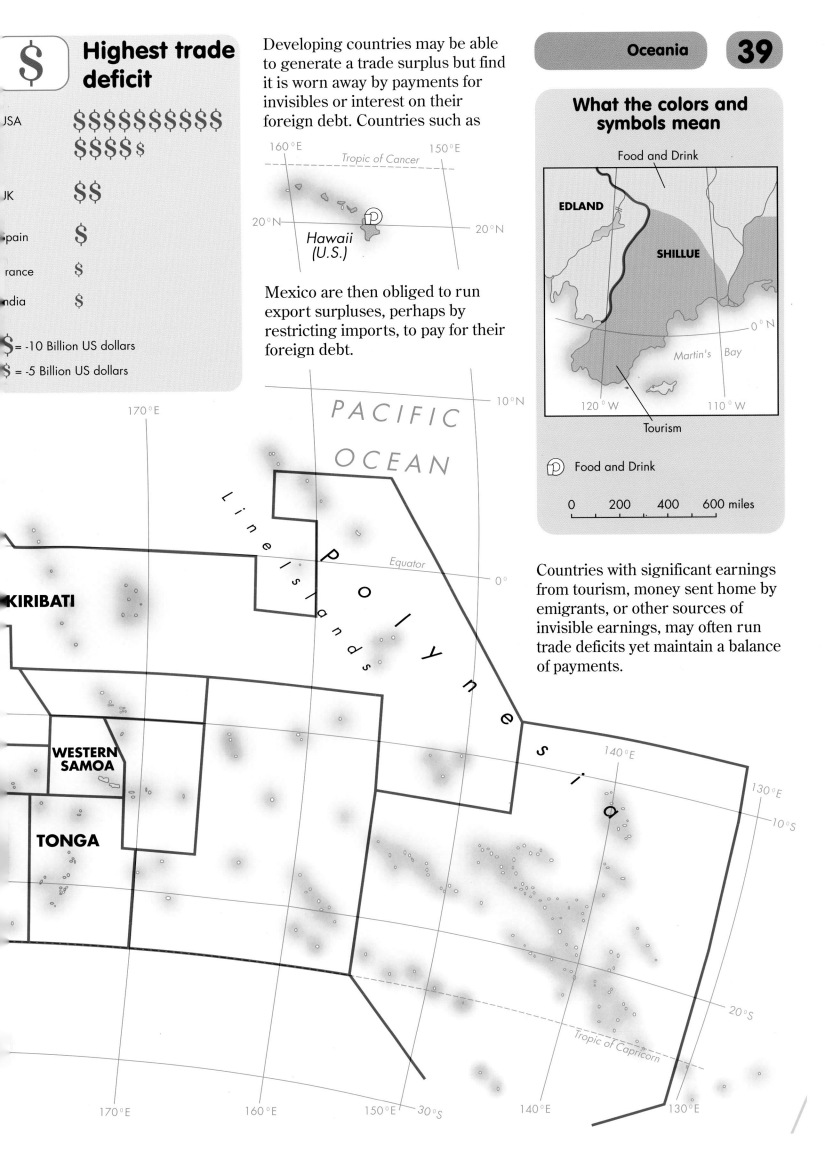

Food and Drink

EDLAND

SHILLUE

Martin's Bay

Tourism

ⓟ Food and Drink

0   200   400   600 miles

Countries with significant earnings from tourism, money sent home by emigrants, or other sources of invisible earnings, may often run trade deficits yet maintain a balance of payments.

Tropic of Cancer

Hawaii (U.S.)

PACIFIC OCEAN

Line islands

Equator

Polynesia

KIRIBATI

WESTERN SAMOA

TONGA

Tropic of Capricorn

The United States is an international economic power, rich in resources, with well-developed industry in all sectors and a big service industry. A leader in technological advancements over a very wide range of fields, a top manufacturer, and also a strong consumer of goods and services, the USA is the most influential of all the world's economies.

Automobile Industry

Most of the world's automobiles come from the USA, Canada, Japan, and Western Europe. Today, approximately 390 million passenger cars are on the roads of the world. In the late 1980s the United States produced more than 7 million cars and 4 million trucks and buses per year. The car industry is also a chief customer of many important industries — steel, lead, and rubber in particular. In the USA, over 12 million people are employed in the industry in some way, including repair shops and service stations.

Most car companies bring out new models every year, and a new model takes three to four years of development. The final stage is the assembly. Cars are put together on assembly lines as a conveyor belt moves along, taking the car from one step to the next. Today production is speeded up by the use of computers and automatic machines, which reduce manufacturing costs and save time and labor.

The United States still accounts for a quarter of world automobile production, but during the 1960s a great deal of growth took place in the industry. In Europe the industries of France, Italy, Spain, and Sweden prospered. The former Soviet Union made an agreement with Italy for the production of Fiats in the USSR. The Australian and Japanese industries thrived, and the Argentine and Brazilian industries expanded their car production. Today, however, it is Japan that produces more cars than any other nation.

Exports are important to car manufacturers. The United States is the largest importer of automobiles. From 1975 to 1980 they imported 16 million automobiles.

Amazing — But True

★ The Union Camp Corporation in the USA is the largest paper mill. It produces enough paper for 200,000 books every day.

★ Cars are tested in a wind tunnel to see the effect of air flow. Smoky air is blown into the wind tunnel at a uniform speed by fans. The pattern of the smoke shows how smoothly the car will travel through the air.

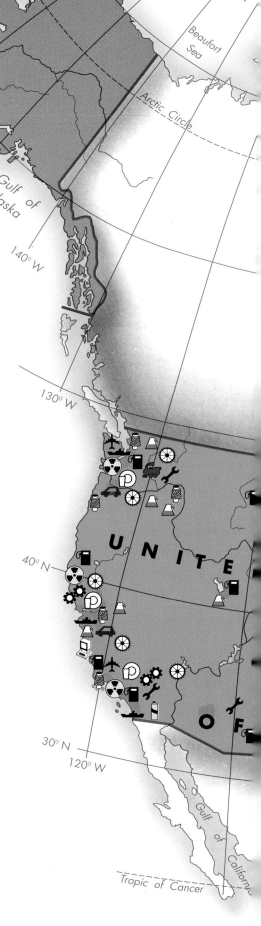

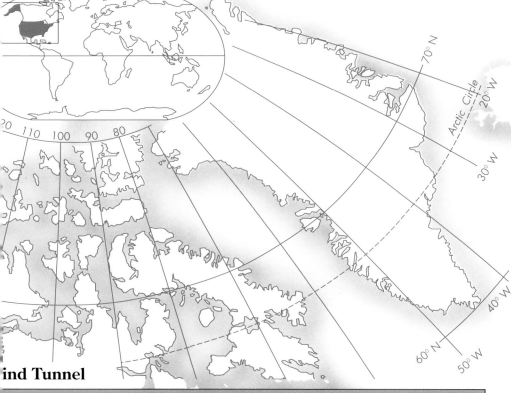

Wind Tunnel

The pattern of wind flowing over a car.

Wind tunnels are used to test a car's aerodynamics.

★ The first company ever to surpass the $1 billion mark in annual sales was the United States Steel Corporation in 1917. Now there are more than 570 corporations with sales exceeding $1 billion, including 272 from the United States.

★ The greatest net profit ever made by any corporation in a year is $7.647 billion, made by American Telephone and Telegraph Co. from October 1981 to September 1982.

What the colors and symbols mean

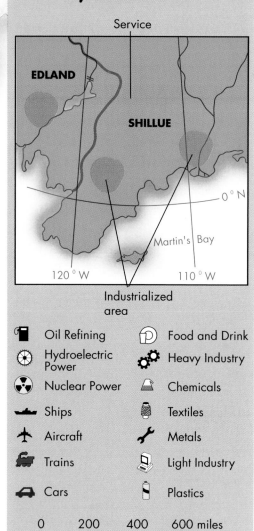

Service

EDLAND

SHILLUE

0° N

Martin's Bay

120° W   110° W

Industrialized area

🛢 Oil Refining		Food and Drink
Hydroelectric Power		Heavy Industry
Nuclear Power		Chemicals
Ships		Textiles
Aircraft		Metals
Trains		Light Industry
Cars		Plastics

0   200   400   600 miles

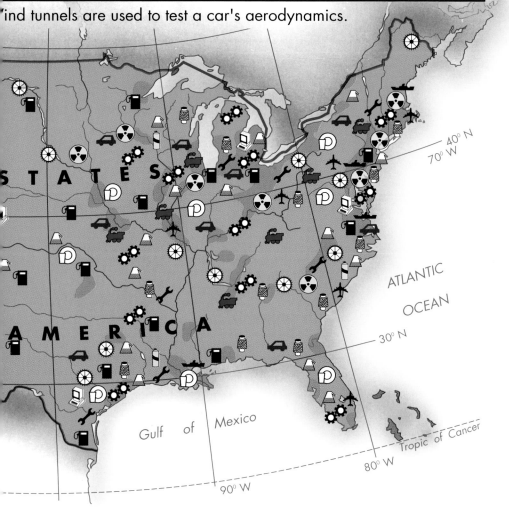

STATES

70° W

40° N

30° N

AMERICA

ATLANTIC OCEAN

Gulf of Mexico

Tropic of Cancer

80° W

90° W

Capital

The material wealth owned by an individual or a business and available for use in the creation of further wealth.

Commerce

All the activities involved in the buying and selling of goods and services.

Commodities

The products of commerce. Units that can be bought or sold in order to gain wealth or that can be used for profit.

Demand

The quantity of goods and services that customers wish to purchase. Demand can be elastic, as when a small change in price causes a large change in demand; or demand inelastic, as when a small change in price does not readily change demand.

Gross Domestic Product (GDP)

GDP is the calculation of the Gross National Product (a measure of the total annual output) of a country, excluding net income from abroad. This figure is used to give an indication of the strength of industry within an economy.

Infrastructure

The basic structures existing in a country: its complex of roads, factories, schools, etc. A sound infrastructure is important for economic growth.

Input

A resource required for industrial production.

Invisible earnings

Invisible items of trade are those that are not goods or products, but rather services such as insurance, banking, transport, and advertising. Invisible earnings are income derived from these items.

Labor

All the people involved in productive work, including management.

Multinational corporation

A large business organization with its headquarters one country and several subsidiaries in other countries. Decision making usually takes place at the head office.

Output

The product of industrial production.

Recession

A temporary depression in economic activity and prosperity. In a recession, demand falls, investment declines, and business failures are more common.

Retail

The sale of goods and services to individual consumers.

Slump

A decline in commercial activity. If a slump is of long duration, it becomes a recession.

Surplus

In economic terms, a surplus is an excess of revenue (income) over expenditure.

Utilities

Public services such as transportation, electricity, or water supply.

Visible income

Income from the sale of goods or products.

Wholesaling

The business of selling goods to retailers in greater quantities than sales to consumers but in smaller quantities than purchases from manufacturers.

Andrews, Kenneth Richmond. *The Concept of Corporate Strategy.*
Rev. ed. Homewood, IL: Richard D. Irwin, 1980.

Boyer, William H. *America's Future : Transition to the 21st Century.*
New York: Praeger, 1984.

Brady, Robert Alexander. *Business as a System of Power.*
Freeport, NY: Books for Libraries Press, 1972.

Hamlin, Scoville, ed. *The Menace of Overproduction.*
Freeport, NY: Books for Libraries Press, 1972.

Harrison, Bennett, and Barry Bluestone. *The Great U-Turn: Corporate Restructuring and the Polarizing of America.*
New York: Basic Books, 1988.

Hirsch, Seev. *Location of Industry and International Competitiveness.*
Oxford: Clarendon Press, 1967.

Hoag, Edwin. *How Business Works.*
Indianapolis: Bobbs-Merrill, 1978.

Miller, E. Willard. *A Geography of Manufacturing.*
Englewood Cliffs, NJ: Prentice Hall, 1962.

Preston, Paul. *Business.*
Englewood Cliffs, NJ: Prentice Hall, 1976.

United Nations. *Industry in a Changing World.*
New York: United Nations, 1983.

This index is designed to help you to find places shown on the maps. The index is in alphabetical order and lists all towns, countries, and physical features. After each entry extra information is given to describe the entry and to tell you which country or continent it is in.

The next column contains the latitude and longitude figures. These are used to help locate places on maps. They are measured in degrees. The blue lines drawn across the map are lines of latitude. The equator is at latitude 0°. All lines above the equator are referred to as °N (north of the equator). All lines below the equator are referred to as °S (south of the equator).

The blue lines drawn from the top to the bottom of the map are lines of longitude. The 0° line passes through Greenwich, London, and is known as the Greenwich Meridian. All lines of longitude join the North Pole to the South Pole. All lines to the right of the Greenwich Meridian are referred to as °E (east of Greenwich), and all lines to the left of the Greenwich Meridian are referred to as °W (west of Greenwich).

The final column indicates the number of the page where you will find the place for which you are searching.

If you want to find out where the Gulf of Thailand is, look it up in the alphabetical index. The entry will read:

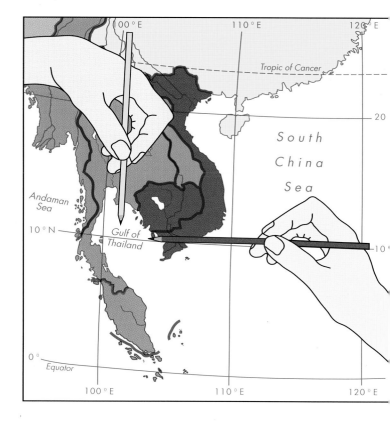

Name, Description	Location		Page
	Lat.	Long.	
Thailand, Gulf of, Asia	11°N	101°E	22

Turn to page 22 in your atlas. The Gulf of Thailand is located where latitude 11°N meets longitude 101°. Place a pencil along latitude 11°N. Now take another pencil and place it along 101°E. Where the two pencils meet is the location of the Gulf of Thailand. Practice finding places in the index and on the maps.

Name, Description	Location		Page
	Lat.	Long.	
A			
Aden, Gulf of, Middle East	12°N	47°E	36
Adriatic Sea, Europe	43°N	15°E	33
Aegean Sea, Greece	35°N	25°E	31
Afghanistan, country in Asia	33°N	65°E	34
Alaska, Gulf of, North America	59°N	145°W	40
Albania, country in Europe	41°N	20°E	31
Algeria, country in Africa	25°N	0°	10
Andaman Sea, Indian Ocean	11°N	96°E	35
Andorra, country in Europe	43°N	2°E	32
Angola, country in Africa	12°S	18°E	12
Antigua and Barbuda,			
island country in Caribbean Sea	18°N	62°W	5
Arabian Sea, Indian Ocean	18°N	60°E	37
Arafura Sea, Southeast Asia	9°S	135°E	24
Aral Sea, Asia	45°N	60°E	28
Argentina,			
country in South America	40°S	68°W	17
Australia, continent and country	23°S	135°E	2
Austria, country in Europe	48°N	15°E	3
B			
Baffin Bay, North America	72°N	65°W	2
Bahamas,			
island country in Atlantic Ocean	25°N	78°W	1
Bahrain, country in Middle East	26°N	51°E	3
Baltic Sea, Europe	57°N	19°E	2
Bangladesh, country in Asia	23°N	90°E	3
Barbados,			
island country in Caribbean Sea	13°N	59°W	1
Barents Sea, Arctic Ocean	73°N	35°E	2
Bass Strait, Australia	40°S	146°E	2
Beaufort Sea, Arctic Ocean	73°N	140°W	2
Belgium, country in Europe	51°N	5°E	3
Belize, country in Central America	17°N	89°W	1
Bellingshausen Sea, Antarctica	67°S	85°W	1
Bengal, Bay of, Indian Ocean	19°N	89°E	3
Benin, country in Africa	10°N	2°E	1

Scott E. Morris an associate professor of geography at the University of Idaho where his current areas of teaching and research interest include mountain geomorphology, field methods, and human impact on the landscape process. Dr. Morris received his Ph.D. from the University of Colorado, Boulder and is published prolifically on the formation and climatic history of mountain landscapes, the effects of wildfire and mineral resource extraction on soil erosion processes, and the influence of water diversion and channel modification on sediment transport.